CARMEN

Georges Bizet
1 8 3 8 - 1 8 7 5

Carmen	Grace Bumbry
Micaëla	Mirella Freni
Frasquita	Eliane Lublin
Mercedes	Viorica Cortez
Don José	Jon Vickers
Escamillo	Kostas Paskalis
Dancaire	Michel Trempont
Remendado	Albert Voli
Morales	Claude Meloni
Zuniga	Bernard Gontcharenko

Conducted by Rafael Frühbeck de Burgos
Orchestra e Coro del Teatro dell'Opera di Roma
Chorus Master: Jean Laforge

CARMEN

CARMEN
Georges Bizet

TEXT BY DAVID FOIL

Additional commentary by William Berger

BLACK DOG
& LEVENTHAL
PUBLISHERS
NEW YORK

The enclosed compact discs ℗ 1970 EMI Records Ltd.
Digital Remastering ℗ 1990 by EMI Records Ltd. Product of EMI-Capitol Music Special Markets,
1750 North Vine Street, Los Angeles, California 90028.

Libretto by Meilhac & Halévy. Reproduced courtesy of Angel/EMI Classics.

Published by
Black Dog & Leventhal Publishers, Inc.
151 West 19th Street
New York, NY 10011

Distributed by
Workman Publishing Company
708 Broadway
New York, NY 10003

Manufactured in China

Cover and interior design by Liz Driesbach.

Cover image © Archives Charmet/Bridgeman Art Library

ISBN: 1-57912-508-5

h g f e d c b a

Library of Congress Cataloging-in-Publication Data available on file.

*E*verybody knows *Carmen*—the great melodies from Georges Bizet's score are among the most recognized melodies in all of music. But the opera itself is a mesmerizing drama of fatal attraction—still startling in its erotic power and violent intensity, still seductive in its imagination and its potent musical personality. The version of the opera you are about to hear is exactly what the composer intended, restoring the work's original theatrical intensity, both as music and as drama.

You will hear the entire opera on the two compact discs included on the inside front and back covers of this book. As you explore the book, you will discover the story behind the opera and its creation, the background of the composer, biographies of the principal singers and conductor, and the opera's text, or libretto, both in the original French and in an English translation. Special commentary has been included throughout the libretto to aid in your appreciation and to highlight key moments in the action and the score.

Enjoy this book and enjoy the music.

CARMEN

$\mathscr{T}$his time I have written a work that is all clarity and vivacity, full of color and melody," the French composer Georges Bizet told a friend late in 1874, adding, "It will be entertaining. Come along—I think you are going to like it."

At that point, Bizet was genuinely pleased with the new opéra comique he had just completed, and was looking forward to its production at the Opéra-Comique in Paris. But this would probably be the last time he felt completely happy about his new

Left: Poster of Emma Calve, a famous early Carmen, circa 1910.
Above: Georges Bizet

Prosper Mérimée

creation, which was called *Carmen*. The rehearsals would be difficult and frustrating; the premiere on March 3, 1875, would be met with apathy. Bizet, who knew he was on to something new in *Carmen*, was bitterly disappointed by this response. Sadly, he did not live to see his work prove a triumphant success only a few years later. He was taken seriously ill shortly after the premiere of *Carmen* and died exactly three months later, early on the morning of June 3, 1875, after the Opéra-Comique gave its thirty-third performance of the opera. Bizet was thirty-six years old.

Carmen has retained more of its allure, magic, and sheer theatrical intensity than almost any other opera in the mainstream repertoire, despite a century of disregard for Bizet's original intentions and a broad popularity that constantly threatens to dump the whole enterprise into the questionable realm of camp. Bizet and his librettists Henri Meilhac and Ludovic Halévy based their work on a dark novella by the French writer Prosper Mérimée. In Mérimée's story, a psychotic soldier, Don José, recounts his obsessive love for an irresistibly carnal creature named Carmen, an obsession that ends with his killing her. In the opera, the bleakness of Mérimée's novella is mitigated somewhat, but the subtle background detail seems to have had a powerful impact on Bizet's music. Making an opera of *Carmen* was apparently his idea and, though he does not have a reputation as a true innovator, he found an uncanny way to reach the bourgeois audience for which he was writing while remaining true to the primal intensity of the material.

Indeed, Georges Bizet's reputation as one of France's greatest composers of the nineteenth century rests almost entirely on *Carmen*. Few composers have shown as much promise as Bizet did as a young man. He was encouraged from an early age by his parents, both of whom were musicians, and entered the Paris Conservatory at the age of nine. As a teenager, he took prizes there in piano and organ performance, and in fugue writing; at the age of nineteen, he was awarded the prestigious Prix de Rome, the seal of approval from the French musical establishment to a young composer. However, Bizet had little interest in writing the kind of music the establishment expected—masses, cantatas, grand symphonic works—and he ran into trouble by trying to write an opera as part of his obligation as the Prix de Rome laureate. (The lighthearted work in question, entitled *Don Procopio*, would not be performed until 1906.) In fact, trouble plagued all of Bizet's many efforts at writing opera. The only other Bizet opera performed today, *Les Pêcheurs de perles* (The Pearl Fishers), completed in 1863, is best known for containing two beautiful arias and a hugely popular duet ("Au fond du temple saint" for tenor and baritone) in an attractive but less than extraordinary score set in an exotic location to a turgid libretto.

An 1878 illustration of *Carmen's* final scene.

The idea of setting *Carmen* as an opera seems to have occurred to Bizet around 1873. His librettists Halévy and Meilhac were a highly esteemed partnership in French opera who wrote, either together or with other collaborators, the librettos for operas by Clement Delibes, Friedrich Flotow, and Jules Massenet and most of Jacques Offenbach's operettas, as well as the plays that inspired the Viennese operettas *Die Fledermaus* and *The Merry Widow*. It seems neither Halévy nor Meilhac—who were consumed with projects they considered more important—thought much of the project or the libretto they fashioned for *Carmen*, and Bizet himself tinkered with the text to bring it to the point where it met his specific demands for the musical score and the drama. The result is a libretto as fine as any in the history of opera, setting the stage for the composition of a score that now seems astonishingly bold.

Bizet's music prior to *Carmen* was unfailingly skillful, attractive, and very much influenced by the work of the respected French composer Charles Gounod, who was his mentor. In his earlier works, Bizet showed a fine gift for melody and an evolving interest in the colors and effects that could be drawn from an orchestra. Yet little of this prepares us for the volatile beauty of the *Carmen* score. The very year he began writing *Carmen*, Bizet had been working on Don Rodrigue, a five-act grand opera about the hero of Spanish history known as El Cid. He abandoned the project because the Opéra burned, temporarily ceasing production and thus eliminating the possibility of a performance; his friend Ernest Guiraud later intimated that the disappearance of the score was a great loss to music. When parts of the *Don Rodrigue* score resurfaced decades later, they revealed another competent but uninspired effort, with little of the genius of *Carmen*, despite a shared Spanish setting.

It is clear that Bizet was both inspired and liberated by the story of *Carmen*,

Composer Charles Gounod (1818-1893) was Bizet's mentor.

resulting in a score that is surprisingly deft, a quality that heightens the work's ambiguous sensuality and mood. Nothing illustrates this lightness of touch more than the breathtaking signature melody that ignites the opera's prelude. Where did this melody come from? It sounds like nothing else in music. Yes, it suggests Spain and a festive scene, but has something else—a wide-eyed, come-what-may excitement, a shocking virility, and a primal intensity that hints at what Carmen instinctively knows and what Don José is afraid to acknowledge. The detail in Bizet's musical plan is extraordinary. Even though one of the score's most famous passages, the habanera sung by Carmen, relies on the melody of the song "El arreglito" by the Spanish songwriter Sebastián de Yradier, Bizet (who thought it was a folk tune) tweaked the rhythm and shape of the melody in a manner that utterly transformed it. The crowning glory of *Carmen* is the final duet, in which the crazed Don José confronts Carmen in a dazzlingly compact fourth act that lasts barely twenty minutes. After the crowd departs for the bullfight, Bizet draws us into the vortex by echoing the signature theme and dragging it down, down, down chromatically, preparing us for what is about to happen. The duet itself is an exquisitely beautiful showpiece for the two singers, heartbreaking in its inevitability and magical in its streamlined eloquence. No less an orchestral master than Richard Strauss once said, "If you want to know how to orchestrate ... study the score of *Carmen*. What wonderful economy, and how every note and rest is in its proper place."

Rosa Ponselle as Carmen.

Why, then, did audiences and critics scratch their heads and recoil when they first heard *Carmen*? Why did Bizet's score confound and infuriate the orchestra that was to play it for the first time? Some of the singers were puzzled, too. The ladies of the chorus, in particular, resented the fact that they were expected to smoke cigarettes and fight onstage (some of them were taken ill in the process), and there was general uneasiness about the sexual candor of the story. However, Bizet's leading singers supported him and threatened to walk out in protest if any kind of censorship was attempted. There is no evidence to support speculation that Bizet was forced against his will to make extensive last-minute cuts and changes in the score. The morning of the premiere of *Carmen*, in fact, the composer was made a chevalier of the Legion of Honor. At last success seemed to be imminent.

It was not to be. Contrary to legend, *Carmen* was not a failure at its premiere, and it did not directly bring about Bizet's death three months later. It can best be described as being neither a flop nor a hit. At the premiere, Bizet reportedly told the young composer Vincent d'Indy, who came to congratulate him and found him pacing outside near the stage door, "I sense defeat. I foresee a definite and hopeless flop. This time I am really sunk." The audience's unenthusiastic, not to say perplexed, response and the negative reviews only reinforced his fears. His mentor Gounod gracelessly insisted that Bizet had stolen the melody for Micaëla's third-act aria from him, and what hadn't been stolen from him and others was mere "sauce without the fish." Opening-night reviews berated Bizet for the

The cigarette girls in front of a wall covered with graffiti in a set designed in 1981 for the San Francisco Opera by Jean-Pierre Ponnelle.

lack of color in his score and—worst of all, to these critics—for a tendency toward Wagnerian techniques. In the wake of the Franco-Prussian war, any suggestion of Richard Wagner's influence was considered in certain quarters to be an insult to French art. "Fed on the enharmonic succulences of the prophets of the music of the future, Bizet seems to have fed his soul on this diet, thereby killing it," one critic wrote, warming up to continue, "Ingenious details in the orchestra, daring dissonances, and instrumental subtleties cannot portray the uterine agonies of Mademoiselle Carmen and the wishes of her wayward lovers ... the music lacks novelty and distinction. There is no plan, no unity in its style ... it is neither dramatic nor scenic."

The chief prophet of the "music of the future," Wagner in fact abhorred *Carmen*. So intense was his dislike that it widened a long-standing breach between him and the philosopher Friedrich Nietzsche that would never heal. Nietzsche found *Carmen* to be a transcendent work of art because the score manages to be "wicked, subtle, and fatalistic" while remaining accessible. "What is good is easy," Nietzsche wrote as his first aesthetic law, "everything divine runs with light feet." The Russian composer Pyotr Ilich Tchaikovsky was an early fan of *Carmen*, too, and insisted that it would soon enjoy world-wide popularity.

No one would dispute the fact that *Carmen* is a masterpiece, and no one has seriously since its apathetic premiere. Yet the "real" *Carmen* has proved elusive for more than the century that it has been in the repertoire of opera houses all over the world. *Carmen* is not an opera, in the strict grand opera sense of the word, but an opéra-comique. *Opéra-comique* is a French term that has no fixed meaning—not all the works so labeled fit the contemporary understanding of comedy—but it has come to refer to an operatic work with comic elements that also has spoken dialogue. In Paris in the midnineteenth century that dialogue distinguished comic opera from the sober, overstuffed grand operas so popular at the Opéra. The theater known as the Opéra-Comique was an altogether less pretentious place than the Opéra, drawing a more bourgeois crowd, and it provided a more relaxed atmosphere for operatic entertainment.

Dome of the Paris Opéra.

By the early 1870s, Bizet had had no success in writing a grand opera that interested the public, and he decided shortly before he set to work on *Carmen* that he should leave that task to others. He wrote *Carmen* for the Opéra-Comique, certain he had found a level on which to communicate with an audience. He crafted a score with a prelude and twenty-seven musical numbers to be linked by spoken dialogue. He personally corrected the proofs on the published score in this form which was published by the Choudens firm in 1875. Yet, for almost one hundred years, the Choudens score was almost never performed.

Much of *Carmen's* popularity rests on an adaptation of the score by Ernest Guiraud, the gifted New Orleans–born,

Paris–based composer who was one of Bizet's best friends. Guiraud created this new version for the Vienna premiere of *Carmen* in October of 1875, replacing Bizet, who had signed the contract to write the recitatives for the production the day before he died. Guiraud made the score more appealing for the opera

Marilyn Horne in the title role.

Geraldine Farrar as Carmen.

house by composing sung recitatives to replace the spoken dialogue, as Bizet himself had been contracted to do. There were some compelling reasons for this change. First of all, the absence of dialogue and the presence of sung recitative made *Carmen* sound more like a grand opera. Second, making it an opera that was fully sung made the performance easier for singers who at the time resented the amount of additional acting they were required to do. Third, opera in the late nineteenth century was not always performed in the language in which it was written, and the distinctively French opéra-

Jose Carreras as the psychotic Don José.

comique—with its pointillistic interplay of the French language both spoken and sung—lost a great deal in translation. But as Guiraud made *Carmen* a more accessible repertory piece and created the version most audiences know, he blunted the razor-sharp double-edged nature of the true opéra-comique Bizet had envisioned.

Carmen is not a pretty story, despite the image of lusty gypsy women with cascades of hair and roses tucked behind their ears that is traditionally associated with the opera. The title character is a woman who is irresistible to men, with a kind of wild dignity all her own. She does whatever she feels like doing, until she makes the fatal mistake of ruining the life of the deeply disturbed Don José. She chooses to live in a world that tolerates her, a world of deception, thievery, cruelty, and violence. Violence is the flip side of beauty in Bizet's opera—in the text, in the action, and in the music itself—and the cruelty of the actions of everyone involved (except Don José's selfless fiancée Micaëla) is stunning. Slightly later, Italians would claim *Carmen* as the forerunner of verismo opera, a vividly realistic style of opera that flourished in Italy around the turn of the twentieth century. *Cavalleria rusticana* and *I pagliacci* are examples of the verismo style and, ultimately, not unlike *Carmen* in their murderous intensity.

But remember Bizet's description: "... all clarity and vivacity ... It will be entertaining." If the Italians thought *Carmen* prefigured *I pagliacci*, it was probably because they knew Carmen from the Guiraud version, where elements of comedy and Bizet's strikingly ambiguous atmosphere had virtually been eliminated. As in a classic American musical comedy, the dialogue between musical numbers in an opéra-comique tends to underscore the characters' humanity, to reveal subtleties and interesting contradictions in their personalities. Instead of the alluring, vampish prima donna that reigns supreme in Guiraud's version, the Carmen of Bizet's opéra-comique is raunchy, sometimes wickedly funny, petty, tantalizingly remote, and unpredictable. Likewise, Bizet's Don José is not the bellowing overgrown boy he can sometimes seem in the Guiraud version, but a deeply conflicted young man full of repressed rage. He is teetering on the brink of insanity, an obsessive-compulsive who becomes a homicidal stalker. In the case of Don José, the opéra-comique version does not make the character lighter but much, much darker.

For all the criticism of Guiraud's version of *Carmen*, it must be said that the quality of his work was excellent. The recitatives are so effective musically that it is sometimes difficult to know what was written by Bizet and what was written by Guiraud. Its effectiveness made it the accepted version, to such an extent that curiosity about the opéra-comique version was left to scholars. However, in 1964, a musicologist named Fritz Oeser

discovered—in a dust-covered, forgotten cupboard at the Opéra-Comique—a conductor's score and orchestral parts that allowed him to reconstruct elements of the score Bizet had not included in the edition published by Choudens in 1875. Oeser's discoveries are fascinating, though Bizet scholar Winton Dean makes a compelling case for viewing the 1875 Choudens score without the Guiraud recitatives as the most authoritative one. If Oeser's new edition raised a controversy, it did reintroduce the idea of presenting *Carmen* in its original form, which is now accepted as the ideal in recordings and in the world's major opera houses. Many recordings of *Carmen* since Oeser's discovery have borrowed from Oeser's edition. But this recording, made in 1969–70, led the way in restoring the primacy of Bizet's 1875 Choudens score. At long last, this is the opera—or rather the opéra-comique—that Bizet meant for the world to hear.

THE STORY OF THE OPERA

Act 1

It is a typical, sleepy day in Seville. Soldiers linger in the square outside the armory, next to a cigarette factory, as the townspeople go about their business. So little is happening that, for the soldiers, the highlight of the guards' watch is the appearance of a shy country girl from Navarre named Micaëla. She is looking for Don José. The corporal Moralès tells her that Don José is due shortly with the relief guard and invites her to wait in the guardhouse. Micaëla recoils, taken aback by the laughing soldiers' interest, and tells Moralès she will return later. Don José arrives with the change of guard and learns of Micaëla's visit.

Zuniga, the lieutenant, kids Don José about his country girlfriend and then asks him what he knows about the cigarette factory girls. Don José insists he pays no attention to them. At that moment, a ringing bell signals a smoking break

A scene from Act I in a production at the Houston Grand Opera.

for the factory girls, which attracts a crowd of young men hoping to catch their attention. The girls enjoy the ritual but, in truth, the men are interested in only one girl—the mysterious and alluring Carmen. Carmen is unfazed by their attention, as they beg her to choose one of them as her lover. She answers to the rhythms of the habanera: love is as untamable as a wild bird, as prone to wandering as a gypsy. Her indifference only intensifies the men's interest.

Carmen tosses an acacia flower to the one man in the square who pays no attention to her—Don José, who is repelled by her boldness yet immediately drawn into her spell. He keeps the flower and quickly hides it in his tunic when Micaëla suddenly appears. She brings Don José a letter and some money from his mother, as well as a kiss; they reminisce about their happiness at home. In the letter, Don José's mother begs him to marry Micaëla and, when his tour of duty ends, return to live near her. Embarrassed by the suggestion, Micaëla leaves, saying they will meet again shortly.

At that moment, a fight breaks out in the cigarette factory. Zuniga, surrounded by screaming girls trying to tell him who started it, sends Don José inside to break it up. Don José emerges with a defiant Carmen, who has slashed the face of another girl. She barely offers a defense of her behavior and, when pressed, only sings derisively in Zuniga's face. He leaves to obtain a warrant for her arrest, charging Don José to guard Carmen. She tricks Don José into a conversation and begins to tease him with the prospect of spending an evening (and

more) with her at the tavern of Lillas Pastia, on the outskirts of Seville. He is unnerved by her attention and eventually agrees to untie her hands so she can escape. When Zuniga returns, Carmen is led away and then suddenly pushes Don José to the ground, humiliating him as she runs away laughing,

Placido Domingo as Don José.

her friends thwarting the soldiers' attempts to recapture her. The lieutenant angrily orders a stunned Don José to be arrested and led away to the brig.

Act 2

Carmen is holding court at Lillas Pastia's with her gypsy friends Frasquita and Mercédès. They sing and dance to the great enjoyment of the soldiers who are pursuing them, led by none other than Zuniga. Carmen is cool to Zuniga, who thinks she is angry at him for trying to have her arrested. She is actually piqued that he had Don José thrown into prison, and she is delighted to hear that the unfortunate soldier is being released that night. They are interrupted by the arrival of Escamillo, the great toreador of Granada, who raises the roof of Lillas Pastia's with a toast after Zuniga buys him a drink. Escamillo is immediately drawn to Carmen, who teases and strings him along with her indifference. Zuniga and his men leave with Escamillo, who tells Carmen he will return for her.

Once the crowd has left, a nervous Lillas Pastia tells Frasquita that the smugglers Dancaïro and Remendado have returned. The gypsy women are delighted, however, and learn that the smugglers need their help in bringing in contraband from Gibraltar. All agree that women are indispensable in such an

enterprise, though Carmen surprises them by saying she will not join them. She is, she says, in love. They laugh at her, but she insists that she is only interested in waiting for Don José's release from prison.

When they hear Don José's voice in the distance, Dancaïro suggests Carmen enlist his aid and have him run away with them. She says she will try, as she hustles the smugglers out of the tavern in order to offer a proper greeting to the young soldier. He becomes jealous when Carmen tells him that Zuniga has been pursuing her. She then calms him by dancing for his enjoyment, accompanied by her castanets. As she dances, he hears a bugle call in the distance, summoning the troops back to the barracks. Don José tells her suddenly he must leave. Carmen explodes in rage, ridiculing his passion and his sense of duty, while berating herself for wasting her time on him.

Don José silences her by producing the acacia flower she tossed him in their first encounter. With a feverish intensity, he tells her that the flower has been his emblem of hope during his imprisonment—proof of his passionate love for her.

Carmen sees her opportunity, scoffing at his assurances and insisting that if he really loved her, he would join her and her friends in their new enterprise. Don José is initially seduced by the idea, then recoils at the thought of being a deserter. He prepares to leave, telling her again how much he loves her, when Zuniga enters to confront him. A hysterical Don José draws his sword on Zuniga. Carmen calls for help from Dancaïro and Remendado. They enter with the other gypsies and tell Zuniga that his timing has been unfortunate. When Carmen again asks Don José to join them, he realizes he now has no choice, and she assures him he will come to love the carefree life of the gypsy.

Carmen (Geraldine Farrar) dances for Don José.

Act 3

Months later, the band of smugglers is still hauling contra-band over the mountains. They pause to rest, as Dancaïro and Remendado go ahead to find out how to slip unnoticed into the next town. Don José, who is clearly miserable, tells Carmen that his mother lives nearby. The charm of their relationship has worn off for Carmen, and she suggests he return home. He flies into a rage at the idea. As a diversion, Frasquita and Mercédès bring out the tarot cards to read their fortunes. The wisdom of the cards amuses them but Carmen is shocked by what they reveal for herself and Don José—death. Believing

what the cards tell her, Carmen knows now what lies in store. Dancaïro and Remendado return, saying they need the women's help in distracting some customs guards. The increasingly despondent Don José is left to guard the

Frasquita (Gloria Lind, left) and Mercedes (Helen Vanni) read the tarot deck.

Scene from a 1990 production of *Carmen* at the Lyric Opera of Chicago.

loot. A guide appears with Micaëla who is searching for Don José. She tells the guide she will proceed alone without fear. Once she is alone, she gives voice to her fears and prays to God for strength. When Micaëla finally sees Don José, she so startles him that he fires his gun without seeing her.

At that moment, with Micaëla cowering unseen, Escamillo enters and tells Don José that the shot just missed him. After introducing himself, he informs Don José that he is looking for Carmen, with whom he is in love. Don José becomes furious and challenges Escamillo to a knife fight. Escamillo, the superior fighter, humors him but then stumbles and suddenly is at Don José's mercy. Only the arrival of Carmen and the other gypsies saves him. Escamillo laughs at the delicious irony of his salvation and invites Carmen and her friends to be his guests at the bullfight in Seville.

Don José, already beside himself, is stunned when the smugglers find Micaëla hiding in the rocks; she tells him that his mother is calling for him. Carmen tells him to go and, though he resists leaving her to Escamillo's favors, he leaves with Micaëla once he learns that his mother is dying and wants to see him one last time. Don José warns Carmen that their affair is not over. Once he leaves, Carmen's fancy turns to the distant sound of Escamillo's singing.

Act 4

Outside the arena in Seville, excitement is growing in anticipation of the great bullfight that will feature Escamillo. A huge crowd awaits the ceremonial procession to the bullring, culminating in the arrival of Escamillo in his toreador regalia, with a resplendent Carmen on his arm. Frasquita and Mercédès have learned that Don José—who is now pursued by the army as a deserter—might be in the vicinity. Before entering the arena in the wake of Escamillo's procession, they try to warn Carmen who dismisses their concern and sends them on into the arena. Alone in the square, she awaits her destiny. Don José emerges from the shadows to tell her that he has not come to harm her, and pleads with her to accept the inevitability of their love. Carmen refuses, and tells him that they are finished. He does not believe her, begging her to take him back. Carmen, distracted by the crowd's cheers for Escamillo, tries to make her way to the bullring but is blocked by Don José who demands to know if she and Escamillo are lovers. Carmen answers that she and the toreador are indeed lovers and that not even the threat of death can make her deny it. The full weight of Carmen's contempt finally hits Don

Carmen meets her destiny in a 1972 production at the Metropolitan Opera.

José. She further insults him by hurling the ring he had given her in his face. Shattered, his ears ringing with the cheers of Escamillo's admirers, Don José attacks Carmen, stabbing her to death. He collapses over her body, admitting his guilt as he professes his love for her.

THE PERFORMERS

GRACE BUMBRY (Carmen) has had a remarkable career as a mezzo-soprano, with occasional forays into the soprano repertory. Born in 1937 in St. Louis, she began singing in church choirs as a little girl and began attending Northwestern University in 1955 as a student of Lotte Lehmann. Bumbry followed Lehmann to the Music Academy of the West in Santa Barbara, California, to continue the study that would shape her as a singer. Her professional debut came in a concert performance in London in 1959; her operatic debut a year later, where she stunned audiences at the Paris Opéra as a last-minute substitute in the role of Amneris in *Aida*. The fact that she was African-American added to the glamour of the debut, and it created a positive furor when Wieland Wagner subsequently signed her to sing the role of Venus in Wagner's *Tannhäuser* at the 1961 Bayreuth Festival. The triumph Bumbry enjoyed there made her an instant celebrity. Her return to the United States brought her to the Kennedy White House and an important concert tour. Her debut at the Chicago Lyric Opera

Grace Bumbry as Carmen.

in 1963 repeated her Bayreuth success as Venus, and her Metropolitan Opera debut was made two years later as Princess Eboli in Verdi's *Don Carlo*. Bumbry's Carmen created a sensation at the 1966 Salzburg Festival under Herbert von Karajan (a production that was filmed), and it became one of her trademark roles. In the early 1970s, Bumbry took advantage of her remarkable range and began singing soprano roles. The title role in Strauss's *Salome* became a particular favorite, as did the fearsome role of Abigaille in Verdi's *Nabucco*, but she also had great success in the title roles of *Tosca* and *Aida*. (She also continued to sing the mezzo-soprano role of Amneris, just as she began to sing Elisabeth as well as Venus in *Tannhäuser*.) Bumbry also sang Bess in the first Metropolitan Opera production of Gershwin's *Porgy and Bess*. In the 1980s, she returned to the great mezzo-soprano roles upon which her reputation rested. Her voice was always remarkable for its expressive richness, power, and extensive range—qualities largely undiminished when she returned to the Metropolitan Opera for a gala appearance in 1996.

JON VICKERS (Don José) exemplified the art of the dramatic tenor throughout his long and remarkable career. Born in 1926 in Prince Albert, Saskatchewan, he emerged from unlikely beginnings in provincial Canada—where he managed F.W. Woolworth stores and served as a purchasing agent for the Hudson Bay Company—to study voice as a scholarship student at the Royal Conservatory of Music in Toronto. Vickers made his professional operatic debut in 1952 as the Duke in *Rigoletto* at the Toronto Opera Festival, and his tremendous promise began to pay off quickly. Within five years, he was singing in London with the Royal Opera, Covent Garden, where he enjoyed great acclaim in 1958 in the title role in Luchino Visconti's legendary production there of Verdi's *Don Carlo*. The heroic profile and unique intensity of Vickers's singing made him a natural candidate for the heldentenor roles in Wagner's music-dramas. Vickers trod carefully around this potentially dangerous repertoire, sticking primarily (and with great success) with Siegmund in Die Walküre, the title role in *Parsifal* and, for a few years, Tristan in *Tristan und Isolde*. He sang Siegmund at the Bayreuth Festival in 1958 and recorded the role twice but avoided the heavier role of Siegfried. Vickers's repertoire was fascinating in its breadth, and it reflected his highly personal, unusually principled approach to his career. He has had little patience with the superficial glamour

Jon Vickers as Don José and Mirella Freni as Michaëla in a 1968–69 production at the Metropolitan Opera.

and politics of the international operatic scene and has been outspoken in his disdain for those who take for granted the moral dimension of art and of being an artist. If these qualities made him a demanding colleague, they also made him an extraordinary one—Vickers delivered as a performer with astonishing consistency and tremendous dramatic power. Earlier in his career, he sang Jason in Luigi Cherubini's *Medea* opposite Maria Callas in thrilling performances with the Dallas Opera that were captured live on tape. His signature roles included Enée in Hector Berlioz's *Les Troyens* (a long-neglected opera he helped popularize), Canio in Ruggero Leoncavallo's *I pagliacci*, Florestan in Beethoven's *Fidelio* and—perhaps most unforgettably—the anguished title characters in Giuseppe Verdi's *Otello* and Benjamin Britten's *Peter Grimes.*

MIRELLA FRENI (Micaëla) was born in 1935 in Modena, a few months earlier than the city's most famous son, Luciano Pavarotti. As infants, the two singers-to-be—who would later become affectionate colleagues—shared the same wet nurse, and their mothers worked in the same cigarette factory. Freni began studying voice with her uncle, making her first public appearance at the age of eleven with another prodigy, the pianist Leone Magiera, who would become her first husband. She made her opera debut in 1955 in Modena as Micaëla in *Carmen*, inaugurating what would be a stellar international stage and recording career of extraordinary range and longevity. After singing several seasons with provincial Italian houses, Freni made strong impressions in debuts with the Amsterdam Opera (1959), London's Covent Garden (1961), and Milan's La Scala (1962), quickly becoming one of Europe's most sought-after lyric sopranos. The role of Mimì in *La Bohème* became her calling card, especially after her performance in the successful 1963 film of Franco Zeffirelli's La Scala production, conducted by Herbert von Karajan. Freni sang Mimì in her debuts at Moscow's Bolshoi Opera (1964) and New York's Metropolitan Opera (1965). She also excelled in such roles as Susanna in *Le nozze di Figaro*, Violetta in *La traviata*, Zerlina in *Don Giovanni*, Marguerite in *Faust*, and Juliette in *Roméo et Juliette*. In the 1970s, when Freni decided to sing heavier roles—a dangerous choice for a lyric soprano—many critics predicted that it would ruin her voice. Bolstered by a steady technique and the sensitive support of conductors such as von Karajan and Riccardo Muti, she was instead acclaimed for bringing a distinctive lyrical warmth to performances and recordings of the title role in *Aida*, Cio-Cio-San in *Madama Butterfly*, Elisabetta in *Don Carlo*, and Leonora in *La forza del destino*. In 1981, she married the Bulgarian bass Nicolai Ghiaurov, a colleague who virtually became her professional partner, notably after Freni began singing Russian roles such as Tatyana in *Eugene Onegin*. In the 1990s, she has been noted for her performances in the demanding prima donna roles of such verismo warhorses as *Adriana Lecouvreur* and *Fedora*.

KOSTAS PASKALIS (Escamillo) began his career with a seven-year stint in the ensemble of the Athens Opera, where he made his professional debut in 1951 in the title role of *Rigoletto* after studying at the Athens Conservatory. Born in 1929 in Lebadea, Greece, he enjoyed a successful debut at the Vienna Staatsoper in 1958, leading to an international career that would last for the next quarter-century. The dramatic intensity of Paskalis's singing was a fine match for the signature baritone roles in the Italian repertoire. He sang frequently at the Vienna Staatsoper and with Berlin's Deutsche Oper, London's Royal Opera at Covent Garden and, in Russia during the Soviet era, with the Bolshoi and Kirov companies. His Metropolitan Opera debut came in 1965 in the role of Carlo in *La forza del destino*. He also sang with other American companies; in 1979, he was reunited with tenor Jon Vickers in a production of Verdi's *Otello* at the Houston Grand Opera. Because Paskalis came to prominence at a time when the baritones Robert Merrill, Tito Gobbi, Ettore Bastianini, Piero Cappuccilli, and Sherrill Milnes were singing, he did not record as frequently as they did. Yet he was an outstanding singer who had particular success with the challenging role of Escamillo in *Carmen*, which he sang (also with Grace Bumbry and Jon Vickers) in Herbert von Karajan's film of his Salzburg Festival production.

RAFAEL FRÜHBECK DE BURGOS (born Rafael Frühbeck) is the son of a German father and a Spanish mother whose training and repertoire are largely reflective of that heritage. Born in the Spanish town of Burgos in 1933, he began his studies as a violinist at the conservatory in Bilbao in 1950. From 1956 until 1958, he studied conducting with Kurt Eichhorn at Munich's Hochschule für Musik, after which he returned to Bilbao to conduct the city's municipal orchestra. Frühbeck de Burgos quickly emerged as Spain's most promising conductor and, in 1962, was named principal conductor of Madrid's Orquesta Nacional de España, a post he held for fifteen years. He simultaneously served as general-musikdirektor of the Düsseldorf Symphony Orchestra (1966–71) and, for two years, as music director of the Montreal Symphony Orchestra (1975–76). In the United States, Frühbeck de Burgos has had a long association with Washington's National Symphony Orchestra, beginning with a stint as principal guest conductor in 1980. He is a frequent guest with orchestras throughout Europe and the United States. His most recent posts have included music director of Tokyo's Yomiuri Nippon Symphony Orchestra and, beginning in 1990, chief conductor of the Vienna Symphony Orchestra. Though he conducts and records the standard orchestral repertoire, he has been especially admired in Spanish music and that with a Spanish flavor, making him an obvious choice for a recording of *Carmen*.

The Libretto

Act 1

DISC NO. 1/TRACK 1

Prelude Wild and indefinable, the thrilling melody that begins the opera's prelude becomes a symbol of the title character. It is heard again only once, in the chorus that greets the bullfighters in Act IV, but its vivid, dancing abandon is the very incarnation of Carmen. There is also a contrasting section that quotes the Toreador Song of Act II (01:01), before the principal melody returns. After a deceptive pause, it is followed by a striking motive that will be heard repeatedly an ominous descending melody (02:07), played against a shuddering orchestra, that represents the inexorable force of fate in Carmen's life. It plunges deeper and deeper as it develops, then rises and builds in tension to an almost unbearable point, where it simply and stunningly snaps—and the opera begins.

The factory scene in a production at the Metropolitan Opera.

Sur la place, chacun passe At the conclusion of the opening chorus, which describes a lazy mid-day scene in the square in Seville and introduces Micaëla, Bizet had written a pantomime, to be sung by Moralès, that he cut almost immediately. It is an amusing, charismatic moment (05:54), written to satisfy an underemployed singer and charmingly done, but because it delays the action it is rarely performed. It was heard for the first time when this recording was released on LP and is included here.

SCENE ONE
Introduction

A square in Seville. On the right, the door of a tobacco factory. At the back, facing the audience, a bridge from one side of the stage to the other, reached from the stage by a winding staircase beyond the factory door. The bridge is open underneath. In front, a guard-house; in front of that, three steps leading to a covered passage. As the curtain rises, a file of soldiers (dragoons of Almanza) are grouped before the guard-house, smoking and looking at the passers-by in the square coming and going. The scene is full of animation.

LES SOLDATS	**SOLDIERS**
Sur la place	On the square
chacun passe,	everyone comes by,
chacun vient, chacun va;	everyone comes and goes;
drôles de gens que ces gens-là!	funny sort of people these!
MORALÈS	**MORALÈS**
A la porte du corps de garde,	At the guard-house door,
pour tuer le temps,	to kill time,
on fume, on jase, l'on regarde	we smoke, gossip, and watch
passer les passants.	the passers-by.
LES SOLDATS ET MORALÈS	**SOLDIERS AND MORALÈS**
Sur la place, *etc.*	On the square, *etc.*

Micaëla enters.

MORALÈS

Regardez donc cette petite
qui semble vouloir nous parler.
Voyez, elle tourne, elle hésite.

LES SOLDATS

A son secours il faut aller!

MORALÈS *(à Micaëla)*

Que cherchez-vous, la belle?

MICAËLA

Moi, je cherche un brigadier.

MORALÈS

Je suis là, voilà!

MICAËLA

Mon brigadier à moi s'appelle
Don José … le connaissez-vous?

MORALÈS

Don José! Nous le connaissons tous.

MICAËLA

Vraiment! Est-il avec vous, je vous prie?

MORALÈS

Il n'est pas brigadier dans notre compagnie.

MICAËLA *(désolée)*

Alors, il n'est pas là?

MORALÈS

Now look at this little lass
who seems to want to speak to us.
Look, she's turning round, she's hesitating.

SOLDIERS

We must go and help her!

MORALÈS *(to Micaëla)*

Whom are you looking for, pretty one?

MICAËLA

I'm looking for a corporal.

MORALÈS

Here I am, look!

MICAËLA

My corporal is called
Don José … do you know him?

MORALÈS

Don José? We all know him.

MICAËLA

Really! Is he with you, please?

MORALÈS

He isn't a corporal in our company.

MICAËLA *(disappointed)*

Then he isn't here?

MORALÈS

Non, ma charmante, il n'est pas là.
Mais tout à l'heure il y sera,
il y sera quand la garde montante
remplacera la garde descendante.

LES SOLDATS ET MORALÈS

Il y sera, *etc.*

MORALÈS

Mais en attendant qu'il vienne,
voulez-vous, la belle enfant,
voulez-vous prendre la peine
d'entrer chez nous un instant?

MICAËLA

Chez vous?

LES SOLDATS ET MORALÈS

Chez nous.

MICAËLA

Non pas, non pas.
Grand merci, messieurs les soldats.

MORALÈS

Entrez sans crainte, mignonne.
je vous promets qu'on aura, pour votre
chère personne,
tous les égards qu'il faudra.

MICAËLA

Je n'en doute pas; cependant
je reviendrai, c'est plus prudent.
Je reviendrai quand la garde montante
remplacera la garde descendante.

MORALÈS

No, my charmer, he isn't here.
But in a few minutes he will be,
he'll be here when the new guard
comes to relieve the old guard.

SOLDIERS AND MORALÈS

He'll be here, *etc.*

MORALÈS

But while you wait for him to come
will you, my pretty child,
take the trouble
to step inside with us for a moment?

MICAËLA

Inside with you?

SOLDIERS AND MORALÈS

Inside with us.

MICAËLA

No, no.
Many thanks, soldiers.

MORALÈS

Don't be afraid to come in, my dear,
I promise you we shall treat
your dear self
with every due respect.

MICAËLA

I don't doubt it; all the same
I'll come back, that's wiser.
I'll be back when the new guard comes to
relieve the old guard.

LES SOLDATS ET MORALÈS	**SOLDIERS AND MORALÈS**
Il faut rester car la garde montante,	You must stay, because the new guard
va remplacer la garde descendante.	is on its way to relieve the old guard.

MORALÈS	**MORALÈS**
Vous resterez!	You'll stay!

MICAËLA	**MICAËLA**
Non pas! non pas!	Indeed I'll not!

surrounding Micaëla

LES SOLDATS ET MORALÈS	**SOLDIERS AND MORALÈS**
Vous resterez!	You'll stay!

MICAËLA	**MICAËLA**
Non pas! Non pas! Non! Non! Non!	Indeed I'll not! No, no, no!
Au revoir, messieurs les soldats!	Goodbye, soldiers!

She escapes and runs off.

MORALÈS	**MORALÈS**
L'oiseau s'envole,	The bird has flown;
on s'en console.	we'll console ourselves.
Reprenons notre passe-temps	Let's resume our pastime
	and watch the folks go by.

SOLDATS	**SOLDIERS**
Sur la place	On the square
chacun passe, *etc.*	everyone comes by, *etc.*

MORALÈS	**MORALÈS**
Drôles de gens! Drôles de gens!	Funny sort of people!
Drôles de gens!	

The movement of the passers-by which had stopped during the foregoing scene has now resumed with a certain animation. Among the people coming and going is an old gentleman with a young lady on his arm … The old gentleman would like to continue his walk, but the young lady is doing all she can to detain him on the square. She seems anxious, uneasy. She looks to right and left. She is expecting someone, and this someone does not come. This pantomime must fit in very exactly with the following verse.

MORALÈS

Attention! Chut! Attention! Taisons-nous!

Voici venir un vieil époux,

Oeil soupçonneux, mine jalouse,

Il tient au bras sa jeune épouse;

L'amant sans doute n'est pas loin;

Il va sortir de quelque coin.

(avec les soldats)

L'amant sans doute n'est pas loin;

Il va sortir de quelque coin.

MORALÈS

Stand by! Sssh! Let's pipe down!

Look, here comes an old husband

with a suspicious eye and a jealous look,

he's holding on to his young wife by the

arm; no doubt the lover's not far off;

he'll pop out of some corner.

(With the soldiers)

No doubt the lover's not far off; he'll pop

out of some corner.

At this moment a young man comes quickly on to the square.

Ah! ah! ah! ah!

Le voilà.

Ha! ha! ha! ha!

There he is.

MORALÈS

Ah! le voilà! oui, le voilà! *etc.*

(avec les soldats)

Voyons comment ce tournera.

MORALÈS

Ah, there he is! Yes, there he is! *etc.*

(With the soldiers)

Let's see how this'll turn out.

The second verse follows and must be faithfully adapted to the scene mimed by the three characters. The young man approaches the old gentleman and the young lady, bows, and exchanges a few words in a low voice, etc.

MORALÈS

imitating the young man's eager greeting

Vous trouver ici, quel bonheur!

MORALÈS

What luck, finding you here!

assuming the old husband's sour-tempered look

| Je suis bien votre serviteur! | Your servant! |

putting on the young man's manner again

| Il salue, il parle avec grâce. | He bows, he turns on the charm. |

then the old husband's expression

| Le vieux mari fait la grimace; | The old husband pulls a face; |

imitating the lady's simpering smiles

| Mais d'un air très encourageant | but the lady is greeting the lover in a very |
| La dame accueille le galant. | encouraging manner. |

At this moment the young man draws from his pocket a note which he shows to the lady. The husband, the wife, and the young blade all three slowly take a little stroll on the square, the young man endeavoring to slip his love-letter to the lady.

MORALÈS

Ils font ensemble quelques pas;	They walk a few steps together;
Notre amoureux, levant le bras,	our lovebird, raising his arm,
fait voir au mari quelque chose,	draws the husband's attention to somthing,

The young man, with one hand, points out something in the sky to the old gentleman, and with the other passes his note to the lady.

Et le mari, toujours morose,	and the husband, still morose,
Regarde en l'air … Le tour est fait,	looks up in the air … The trick has worked,
car la dame a pris le billet!	for the lady has taken the note.
Et voilà! Et voilà! Ah! ah!	And that's that! that's that! Ha! Ha!
On voit comment ça tournera!	We see how that'll turn out!
(avec les soldats)	(with the soldiers)

On voit comment ça tournera!   We see how that'll turn out!

Ah! ah! ah! ah!   Ha! ha! ha! ha!

On voit comment ça tournera! *etc.*   We see how that'll turn out! *etc.*

SCENE TWO
March and Chorus of Street Boys

A military march of bugles and fifes is heard in the distance. The relief guard is arriving. The old gentle-man and the young man exchange a cordial handshake, and the young man bows respectfully to the lady. An officer comes out of the guard-house. Soldiers take their muskets and form up in front of the guard-house. The passers-by gather in a group to watch the parade. The military march comes nearer and nearer. At last the relief guard emerges and crosses the bridge. First, two bugles and two fifes. Then a band of street urchins. Behind the children, Lieutenant Zuniga and Corporal Don José, then the troopers.

DISC NO. 1/TRACK 3

This chipper boys's chorus with the unforgettable melody (augmented by tweeting piccolos) forms a severe contrast with the music we will hear associated with Carmen and Don José.

CHOEUR DES GAMINS	CHORUS OF STREET BOYS
Avec la garde montante,	Right beside the relief guard,
Nous arrivons, nous voilà.	here we come, here we are!
Sonne, trompette éclatante!	Blow out, loud trumpet!
Taratata, taratata!	Taratata, taratata!
Nous marchons la tête haute	We march with head erect
Comme de petits soldats,	like little soldiers,
Marquant sans faire de faute,	keeping time with no mistakes—
Une, deux, marquant le pas.	one, two—keeping step.
Les épaules en arrière	Shoulders back
Et la poitrine en dehors,	and chest well out,
Les bras de cette maniére	arms this way

| Tombant tout le long du corps. | straight down beside the body. |
| Avec la garde montante, *etc.* | Right beside the relief guard, *etc.* |

The relief guard halts facing the guard going off duty. The officers salute with their swords and begin to talk in low voices. The sentries are changed.

MORALÈS (*à Don José*)

Il y a une jolie fille qui est venue to demander. Elle a dit qu'elle reviendrait....

MORALÈS (*to Don José*)

There's a pretty girl been asking for you. She said she'd come back....

JOSÉ

Une jolie fille?

JOSÉ

A pretty girl?

MORALÈS

Oui, et gentiment habillée, une jupe bleue, des nattes tombant sur les épaules....

MORALÈS

Yes, and nicely dressed, a blue skirt, plaits down over her shoulders....

JOSÉ

C'est Micaëla. Ce ne peut être que Micaëla.

JOSÉ

It's Micaëla. It can only be Micaëla.

MORALÈS

Elle n'a pas dit son nom.

MORALÈS

She didn't give her name.

REPRISE DU CHOEUR DES GAMINS

Et la garde descendante
Rentre chez elle et s'en va.
Sonne, trompette éclatante,
Taratata, taratata!
Nous marchons la tête haute
Comme de petits soldats, *etc.*

CHORUS OF STREET BOYS (*reprise*)

And the old guard
goes off home to barracks.
Blow out, loud trumpet!
Taratata, taratata!
We march with head erect
like little soldiers, *etc.*

Soldiers, urchins, and idlers go off at the back; the sound of chorus, fifes, and bugles grows fainter. The commander of the new guard, during this time, inspects his men silently. When the chorus of street boys can no longer be heard, the soldiers are dismissed and enter the guard-house. Don José and Zuniga remain.

ZUNIGA

Dites-moi, brigadier? Qu'est-ce que c'est
que ce grand bâtiment?

JOSÉ

C'est la manufacture de tabacs …

ZUNIGA

Ce sont des femmes qui travaillent là? …

JOSÉ

Oui, mon lieutenant. Elles n'y sont pas
maintenant tout à l'heure, après leur dîner,
elles vont revenir. Il y aura du monde pour
les voir passer.

ZUNIGA

Il y en a de jeunes?

JOSÉ

Mais oui, mon lieutenant.

ZUNIGA

Et de jolies?

JOSÉ *(en riant)*

Je le suppose … je n'ai les ai jamais beaucoup regardées …

ZUNIGA

Allons donc! …

JOSÉ

… ces Andalouses me font peur, toujours
à railler … jamais un mot de raison…

ZUNIGA

Tell me, corporal, what's that great
building?

JOSÉ

It's the tobacco factory …

ZUNIGA

It's women who work there? …

JOSÉ

Yes, sir. They're not there now presently,
after their dinner, they'll come back.
Everyone'll be here to see them go by.

ZUNIGA

There are young ones?

JOSÉ

Why yes, sir.

ZUNIGA

And pretty ones?

JOSÉ *(laughing)*

I suppose so … I've never taken much
notice of them …

ZUNIGA

Get away with you! …

JOSÉ

These Andalusian girls frighten me …
always making fun of you … never a word
of sense …

ZUNIGA

Et puis nous avons un faible pour les jupes bleues et pour les nattes tombant sur les épaules …

JOSÉ *(riant)*

Ah! mon lieutenant a entendu ce que disait Moralès?

ZUNIGA

Oui …

JOSÉ

Je ne le nierai pas … la jupe bleu, les nattes, c'est le costume de la Navarre … ça me rappelle le pays …

ZUNIGA

Vous êtes Navarrais?

JOSÉ

Et vieux chrétien. Malheureusement, j'aimais trop jouer à la paume … Un jour, un gars me chercha querelle; j'eus encore l'avantage, mais cela m'obligea de quitter le pays. Je me fis soldat! Ma mère me suivit et vint s'établir à dix lieues de Séville … avec la petite Micaëla…

ZUNIGA

And then we've got a weakness for blue skirts and for pigtails down over the shoulders …

JOSÉ *(laughing)*

Ah, sir, so you heard what Moralès said?

ZUNIGA

Yes …

JOSÉ

I won't deny it … blue skirt, pigtails, it's the dress of Navarra … that reminds me of home …

ZUNIGA

You're from Navarra?

JOSÉ

And from an old Christian family. Unfortunately I was too fond of playing paume* … one day a lad picked a quarrel with me; I came off best again, but this forced me to leave the country. I went for a soldier! My mother followed me and came to settle ten leagues from Seville … with the little Micaëla.

DISC NO. 1/TRACK 4

The orchestra plays as José is still talking, expanding into a lazy melody as the young men admire the girls of the cigarette factory. The girls themselves sing a languid melody (02:18), the idleness of their break time and the afternoon heat, as well as the patterns of their smoke, depicted by the woodwinds.

* A kind of fives.

ZUNIGA

Et quel âge a-t-elle, la petite Micaëla?

ZUNIGA

And how old is the little Micaëla?

JOSÉ

Dix-sept ans.

JOSÉ

Seventeen.

ZUNIGA

Il fallait dire cela tout de suite … Je comprends maintenant pourquoi vous ne pouvez pas me dire si les ouvrières sont jolies ou laides.

ZUNIGA

You should have said that at once…. Now I understand why you can't tell me whether the factory-girls are pretty or ugly.

The factory bell is heard.

JOSÉ

Voici la cloche qui sonne, mon lieutenant, vous allez pouvoir juger pour vous-même… Quant à moi, je vais faire une chaîne pour attacher mon épinglette.

JOSÉ

There's the bell ringing, sir, you'll be able to judge for yourself…. As for me, I'm going to make a chain for fixing my priming-pin.

SCENE THREE
Chorus of Cigarette Girls

The square fills up with young men who have come to intercept the cigarette girls. The soldiers come out of the guard-house. Don José sits down on a seat, and remains quite indifferent to all the comings and goings, working on a little chain for his priming-pin.

JEUNES GENS

La cloche a sonné; nous, des ouvrières
nous venons ici guetter le retour;
et nous vous suivrons, brunes cigarières,
en vous murmurant des propos d'amour!

YOUNG MEN

The bell has rung; we've come here to
catch the factory-girls on their way back;
and we'll follow you, dark-haired cigarette
girls, murmuring words of love to you!

At this point the girls appear, smoking cigarettes.

LES SOLDATS

Voyez-les! Regards impudents,

mines coquettes,

fumant toutes du bout des dents la cigarette.

LES CIGARIÈRES

Dans l'air, nous suivons des yeux

la fumée, la fumée,

qui vers les cieux

monte, monte parfumée.

Cela monte gentiment

à la tête, à la tête,

toute doucement

cela vous met l'âme en fête!

Le doux parler des amants,

c'est fumée!

Leurs transports et leurs serments,

c'est fumée!

Dans l'air, nous suivons des yeux

la fumée, *etc.*

LES SOLDATS

Mais nous ne voyons pas la Carmencita!

Carmen enters

LES CIGARIÈRES ET LES JEUNES GENS

La voilà!

La voilà!

Voilà la Carmencita!

SOLDIERS

Look at them! Impudent glances,

saucy airs,

all of them puffing away at a cigarette.

CIGARETTE GIRLS

We gaze after the smoke

as it rises in the air,

sweet-smelling,

towards the skies.

Gracefully it mounts

to your head,

so gently

it exhilarates you!

Lovers' soft talk—

it's smoke!

Their raptures and promises—

smoke!

We gaze after the smoke

as it rises, *etc.*

SOLDIERS

But we don't see La Carmencita!

CIGARETTE GIRLS AND YOUNG MEN

There she is!

There she is!

There's La Carmencita!

She has a bunch of acacia flowers at her bodice, and an acacia flower in the corner of her mouth. The young men come in with Carmen. They follow her, surround her, talk to her. She flirts with them in an offhand fashion. Don José looks up. He glances at Carmen and then quietly resumes his work.

LES JEUNES GENS	YOUNG MEN
Carmen! sur tes pas, nous nous pressons tous!	Carmen, we all throng after you!
Carmen! sois gentille, au moins réponds-nous	Carmen, be kind, answer us at least,
et dis-nous quel jour tu nous aimeras!	and tell us when you're going to love us!

DISC NO. 1/TRACK 5

Quand je vous aimerai? ... L'amour est un oiseau rebelle (Habanera) **Carmen is introduced to the stage with a rushing melody in the strings suggesting a dangerous character. Actually, the melody is the "Fate" motif heard in the prelude but played three times faster. This leads into the most famous solo of the opera, Carmen's "Habanera" (00:31). A habanera is not a Spanish but a Cuban musical form. It was inspired and inventive for Bizet to borrow the basic melody, a Hispanic-American dance rhythm, from a song popular in France at that time. The gently rocking habanera suggests a mysterious allure that reaches back into ancient and elusive cultures, which sound part gypsy and part Moorish to the modern listener.**

CARMEN *(regardent Don José)*	CARMEN *(with a glance at Don José)*
Quand je vous aimerai?	When I'm going to love you?
Ma foi, je ne sais pas.	My word, I don't know.
Peut-être jamais, peut-être demain;	Perhaps never, perhaps tomorrow;
mais pas aujourd'hui, c'est certain.	but not today, that's certain.

Grace Bumbry in a 1968–69 production of *Carmen* at the Metropolitan Opera.

SCENE FOUR
Habanera

CARMEN

L'amour est un oiseau rebelle
que nul ne peut apprivoiser,
et c'est bien en vain qu'on l'appelle,
s'il lui convient de refuser.
Rien n'y fait, menace ou prière,
l'un parle bien, l'autre se tait;
et c'est l'autre que je préfère
il n'a rien dit, mais il me plaît.
L'amour! *etc.*

CHOEUR

L'amour est un oiseau rebelle, *etc.*

CARMEN

L'amour est enfant de bohème,
il n'a jamais connu de loi
Si tu ne m'aimes pas, je t'aime;
si je t'aime, prends garde à toi! *etc.*

CHOEUR

Prends garde à toi! *etc.*
L'amour est enfant de bohème, *etc.*

CARMEN

L'oiseau que to croyais surprendre
battit de l'aile et s'envola—
l'amour est loin, tu peux l'attendre;
tu ne l'attends plus il est là!
Tout autour de toi vite, vite,
il vient, s'en va, puis il revient—
tu crois le tenir, il t'évite,

CARMEN

Love is a rebellious bird
that no one can tame,
and it's quite useless to call him
if it suits him to refuse.
Nothing moves him, neither threat nor
plea, one man speaks freely, the other keeps
mum; and it's the other one I prefer
he's said nothing, but I like him.
Love! *etc.*

CHORUS

Love is a rebellious bird, *etc.*

CARMEN

Love is a gypsy child,
he has never heard of law.
If you don't love me, I love you;
if I love you, look out for yourself! *etc.*

CHORUS

Look out for yourself! *etc.*
Love is a gypsy child, *etc.*

CARMEN

The bird you thought to catch unawares
beat its wings and away it flew—
love's far away, and you can wait for it;
you wait for it no longer—and there it is.
All around you, quickly, quickly,
it comes, it goes, then it returns—
you think you can hold it, it evades you,

tu crois l'éviter, il te tient.	you think to evade it, it holds you fast.
L'amour! *etc.*	Love! *etc.*

CHOEUR

Tout autour de toi, *etc.*

CHORUS

All around you, *etc.*

CARMEN

L'amour est enfant de bohème,
il n'a jamais connu de loi.
Si tu ne m'aimes pas, je t'aime;
si je t'aime, prends garde à toi!
Si tu ne m'aimes pas, je t'aime, *etc.*

CARMEN

Love is a gypsy child,
he has never heard of law.
If you don't love me, I love you;
if I love you, look out for yourself!
If you don't love me, I love you, *etc.*

CHOEUR

Prends garde à toi! *etc.*
L'amour est enfant de bohème, *etc.*

CHORUS

Look out for yourself! *etc.*
Love is a gypsy child, *etc.*

SCENE FIVE
Scene

DISC NO. 1/TRACK 6

Carmen! sur tes pas, nous nous pressons tous! **In the moment following the habanera, Carmen ponders which man might be the recipient of her acacia flower. She looks beyond the men who desire her to one who does not, the otherwise engaged Don José (00:13). As she approaches him, the accompaniment is reduced to a sustained note in the violas (00:41), followed by a dissonant slap of a chord as Carmen tosses the flower at José, laughs, and runs away.**

JEUNES GENS

Carmen! sur tes pas, nous nous pressons
tous! Carmen! sois gentille, au moins
réponds-nous!

YOUNG MEN

Carmen, we all throng after you!
Carmen, be kind, answer us at least!

A pause. The young men surround Carmen, who looks at them one by one. Then she breaks through the circle and goes straight to Don José, who is still busied with his little chain.

CARMEN

Qu'est-ce tu fais là? …

JOSÉ

Je fais une chaîne pour attacher mon épin-glette.

CARMEN

Ton épinglette, vraiment! Ton épinglette… épinglier de mon âme …

CARMEN

What are you up to there? …

JOSÉ

I'm making a chain to fix my priming-pin.

CARMEN

Your priming-pin, really! Your priming pin. … Pin-maker of my heart …

Carmen throws the acacia flower at Don José. He jumps up. The flower has fallen at his feet. Outburst of general laughter.

LES CIGARIERÈS

surrounding Don José

L'amour est enfant de bohème, *etc.*

CIGARETTE GIRLS

Love is a gypsy child, *etc.*

The factory bell rings again. Carmen and the other cigarette girls run into the factory. Exeunt young men, etc. The soldiers go into the guard-house, followed by the lieutenant, who had been chatting to two or three of the girls. Don José is left alone.

JOSÉ

Qu'est-ce cela veut dire, ces façons-là? … Quelle effronterie!

JOSÉ

What's all that mean?—all those carryings-on? … What shamelessness!

He looks at the acacia flower on the ground at his feet. He picks it up.

Avec quelle adresse elle me l'a lancée, cette fleur…

How cleverly she threw it at me, this flower …

Enrico Caruso as Don José.

He smells the flower.

S'il y a des sorcières, cette fille-là en est une.   If there are witches, that girl is one.

Enter Micaëla

DISC NO. 1/TRACK 7

Monsieur mon brigadier? ... Ma mère, je la vois **The duet of Don José and Micaëla brings some relief after the raw sexual tension that has been building steadily since the curtain rose on Act I. The music is unabashedly sweet, even bucolic in its sound (00:19), reflecting Don José's sentimental feelings for home, for his mother (00:35), and for the virginal Micaëla who has come to find him. It is interesting to note how the orchestration for Don Josés music tends to adapt to that of the character he is addressing in a given moment—an apt psychological touch by Bizet. Like the rest of the music in the score associated with Micaëla (a character who does not appear in Merimée's novella), this duet is in a style typical of the French opera then—fluently melodic and tender in its expression (03:46), yet not as overtly passionate as the Italian style.**

MICAËLA

Monsieur le brigadier?

JOSÉ

hurriedly concealing the acacia flower

Qu'est-ce que c'est? … Micaëla! … Tu
viens de là-bas? …

MICAËLA

C'est votre mère qui m'envoie…

MICAËLA

Corporal?

JOSÉ

What's this? … Micaëla! … You've come
from back there? …

MICAËLA

It's your mother who sends me …

SCENE SIX
Duet

JOSÉ

Parle-moi de ma mère!

MICAËLA

J'apporte de sa part, fidèle messagère,
cette lettre…

JOSÉ

Une lettre! *etc.*

MICAËLA

Et puis un peu d'argent
pour ajouter à votre traitement.
Et puis …

JOSÉ

Tell me about my mother!

MICAËLA

A faithful messenger, I bring from her this
letter …

JOSÉ

A letter! *etc.*

MICAËLA

And then a little money to add to your pay.
And then …

JOSÉ

Et puis?

MICAËLA

Et puis … vraiment je n'ose,
et puis encore une autre chose
qui vaut mieux que l'argent
qui pour un bon fils
aura sans doute plus de prix.

JOSÉ

Cette autre chose, quelle est-elle?
Parle donc.

MICAËLA

Oui, je parlerai;
ce que l'on m'a donné
je vous le donnerai.
Votre mère avec moi sortait de la chapelle,
et c'est alors qu'en m'embrassant;
"Tu vas", m'a-t-elle dit, "t'en aller à la ville;
la route n'est pas longue, une fois à Séville,
tu chercheras mon fils, mon José, mon
enfant.
Et tu lui diras que sa mère
songe nuit et jour à l'absent,
qu'elle regrette et qu'elle espère,
qu'elle pardonne et qu'elle attend.
Tout cela, n'est-ce pas, mignonne,
de ma part tu le lui diras;
et ce baiser que je te donne
de ma part tu le lui rendras."

JOSÉ *(très ému)*

Un baiser de ma mère!

JOSÉ

And then?

MICAËLA

And then … really, I dare not,
and then yet another thing
worth more than money
and which a good son will surely value
higher.

JOSÉ

This other thing, what is it?
Tell me, then.

MICAËLA

Yes, I'll tell you;
what was given to me
I'll give to you.
Your mother and I were coming out of the
chapel,
And then, as she kissed me,
"You will go to town," she said.
"it's not far; once in Seville
you'll seek out my son, my José, my boy.
And you'll tell him that his mother
thinks night and day of her absent one,
that she grieves and hopes,
that she forgives and waits.
All that, little one,
you'll tell him from me, won't you;
and this kiss that I'm giving you
you'll give him from me."

JOSÉ *(very moved)*

A kiss from my mother!

MICAËLA

Un baiser pour son fils!
José, je vous le rends,
comme je l'ai promis.

MICAËLA

A kiss for her son!
José, I give it to you
as I promised.

Micaëla raises herself on tiptoe and gives Don José a frank, motherly kiss. José, very moved, lets her. He gazes into her eyes. There is a moment of silence.

JOSÉ

Ma mère, je la vois!
Oui, je revois mon village!
O souvenirs d'autrefois,
doux souvenirs du pays!
Doux souvenirs du pays!
O souvenirs chéris!
Vous remplissez mon coeur
de force et de courage!
O souvenirs chéris!
Ma mère, je la vois,
je revois mon village!

JOSÉ

I see my mother!
Yes, I see my village again!
O memories of bygone days,
sweet memories of home!
Sweet memories of home!
O precious memories!
You put back strength
and courage into my heart!
O precious memories!
I see my mother,
I see my village again!

MICAËLA

Sa mère, il la revoit!
Il revoit sa village!
O souvenirs d'autrefois!
Souvenirs du pays!
Vous remplissez son coeur
de force et de courage!
O souvenirs chéris!
Sa mère, il la revoit,
il revoit son village!

MICAËLA

He sees his mother again!
He sees his village again!
O memories of bygone days!
Memories of home!
You put back strength
and courage into his heart!
O precious memories!
He sees his mother again,
he sees his village again!

JOSÉ

his eyes fixed on the factory

Qui sait de quel démon
j'allais être la proie!
Même de loin, ma mère me défend,
et ce baiser qu'elle m'envoie
écarte le péril et suave son enfant!

MICAËLA

Quel démon? quel péril?
Je ne comprends pas bien.
Que veut dire cela?

JOSÉ

Rien! Rien!
Parlons de toi, la messagère.
Tu vas retourner au pays?

MICAËLA

Oui, ce soir même
demain je verrai votre mère.

JOSÉ

Tu la verras!
Et bien, tu lui diras
que son fils l'aime et la vénère
et qu'il se repent aujourd'hui;
il veut que là-bas sa mère
soit contente de lui!
Tout cela, n'est-ce pas, mignonne,
de ma part, tu le lui diras,
et ce baiser que je te donne,
de ma part tu le lui rendras.

He kisses her.

JOSÉ

Who knows into what demon's clutches
I was about to fall!
Even from afar my mother protects me
and this kiss she sent me
wards off the peril and saves her son!

MICAËLA

What demon? What peril?
I don't quite understand.
What do you mean by that?

JOSÉ

Nothing! Nothing!
Let's talk about you, the messenger.
You're going back home?

MICAËLA

Yes, this very evening
tomorrow I shall see your mother.

JOSÉ

You'll be seeing her!
Well then, you'll tell her—
that her son loves and reveres her
and that today he is repentant;
he wants his mother back there
to be pleased with him!
All this, my sweet,
you'll tell her from me, won't you, and this
kiss that I give you
you'll give her from me.

MICAËLA

Oui, je vous le promets, de la part de son fils
José je le rendrai comme je l'ai promis.

MICAËLA

Yes, I promise you; from her son
José I shall give it as I have promised.

JOSÉ

Ma mère, je la vois! *etc.*

JOSÉ

I see my mother! *etc.*

MICAËLA

Sa mère, il la revoit! *etc.*

MICAËLA

He sees his mother again! *etc.*

DISC NO. 1/TRACK 8

Attends un peu maintenant In the original production, the chorus that describes the fight in the cigarette factory (00:25) left the ladies of the Opéra-Comique's original ensemble in a state of frenzy. Already tested by the smoking chorus that introduced them earlier, they were not only required to sing this particularly intricate ensemble, they had to be physically boisterous as well. (Their preferred manner of performing was to stand facing forward and simply sing.) It is a stunning moment, as bloodthirsty and gritty as anything in Italian verismo opera, with Bizet neatly catching the visceral, almost carnal excitement (02:30) the fight has aroused in its witnesses.

JOSÉ

Attends un peu maintenant… je vais lire
sa lettre …

JOSÉ

Wait a bit now… I'm going to read her letter …

MACAËLA

Je viens de me rappeler que votre mère m'a
chargée de quelques petits achats …

MICAËLA

I've just remembered that your mother asked
me to make a few small purchases for her …

JOSÉ

Attends un peu …

JOSÉ

Wait a little while …

MICAËLA

Non, non … je reviendrai, j'aime mieux
cela … je reviendrai, je reviendrai …

MICAËLA

No, no … I'll come back, I'd rather do
that … I'll come back, I'll come back …

She goes out.

JOSÉ

reading

"Il n'y en a pas qui t'aime davantage …
et si tu voulais …" Oui, ma mère, oui,
j'épouserai Micaëla. Quant à cette bohèmi-
enne, avec ses fleurs qui ensorcellent …

*Just as he is about to tear the flower from his tunic, an uproar begins in the factory. Zuniga comes on stage,
followed by soldiers.*

ZUNIGA

Eh bien! eh bien! qu'est-ce qui arrive?

SCENE SEVEN
Chorus

PREMIER GROUPE DE FEMMES

Au secours! Au secours!
N'entendez-vous pas?

DEUXIÈME GROUPE DE FEMMES

Au secours! Au secours!
Messieurs les soldats!

PREMIER GROUPE DE FEMMES

C'est la Carmencita!

DEUXIÈME GROUPE DE FEMMES

Non, non, ce n'est pas elle!
Pas du tout!

JOSÉ

"There's not one of them who loves you
more … and if you wanted to …" Yes,
mother, yes, I'll marry Micaëla. As for that
gypsy with her flowers that bewitch …

ZUNIGA

Well now, well, what's happening? …

FIRST GROUP OF GIRLS

Help! Help!
Can't you hear?

SECOND GROUP OF GIRLS

Help! Help!
You soldiers!

FIRST GROUP OF GIRLS

It's Carmencita!

SECOND GROUP OF GIRLS

No, no, it's not her!
Not a bit of it!

PREMIER GROUPE DE FEMMES	FIRST GROUP OF GIRLS
C'est elle! Si fait, si fait, c'est elle!	It's her! It is, it is! It's her!
Elle a porté les premiers coups!	She started the fighting!

DEUXIÈME GROUPE DE FEMMES	SECOND GROUP OF GIRLS
Ne les écoutez pas!	Don't listen to them!

TOUTES LES FEMMES	ALL THE GIRLS

surrounding Zuniga

Ecoutez-nous, monsieur!	Listen to us, sir!
Ecoutez-nous! *etc.*	Listen to us! *etc.*

DEUXIÈME GROUPE DE FEMMES	SECOND GROUP OF GIRLS

pulling the officer to their side

La Manuelita disait,	Manuelita said, and kept saying
et répétait à voix haute	at the top of her voice,
qu'elle achèterait sans faute	that she'd make sure she bought
un âne que lui plaisait.	a donkey that pleased her.

PREMIER GROUPE DE FEMMES	FIRST GROUP OF GIRLS
Alors la Carmencita,	Then Carmencita,
railleuse à son ordinaire,	in her usual mocking way,
dit "Un âne, pourquoi faire?	said "A donkey? What for?
Un balai te suffira."	A broom will do for you."

DEUXIÈME GROUPE DE FEMMES	SECOND GROUP OF GIRLS
Manuelita riposta	Manuelita retorted,
et dit à sa camarade	and said to her friend
"Pour certaine promenade,	"For a certain ride
mon âne te servira!—"	my donkey will be useful to you!—"

PREMIER GROUPE DE FEMMES	FIRST GROUP OF GIRLS

PREMIER GROUPE DE FEMMES

"—Et ce jour-là tu pourras
à bon droit faire la fière;
deux laquais suivront derrière,
t'émouchant à tour de bras!"

FIRST GROUP OF GIRLS

"—And on that day you'll be able
to play the lady in your own right;
two lackeys will follow behind
keeping flies off as best they can!"

TOUTES LES FEMMES

Là-dessus, toutes les deux
se sont prises aux cheveux!

ALL THE GIRLS

Thereupon they both started
to pull each other's hair out!

ZUNIGA

Au diable tout ce bavardage!
Prenez, José, deux hommes avec vous
et voyez là-dedans qui cause ce tapage.

ZUNIGA

To the devil with all this chatter!
José, take two men in with you
and see who's causing all this commotion.

Don José takes two men with him. The soldiers go into the factory. All this while the girls are pushing and arguing among themselves.

PREMIER GROUPE DE FEMMES

C'est la Carmencita! *etc.*

FIRST GROUP OF GIRLS

It's Carmencita! *etc.*

DEUXIÈME GROUPE DE FEMMES

Non, non, ce n'est pas elle! *etc.*

SECOND GROUP OF GIRLS

No, no! It's not her! *etc.*

ZUNIGA

Holà!
Eloignez-moi toutes ces femmes-là!

ZUNIGA

Stop!
Rid me of all these women!

TOUTES LES FEMMES

Monsieur! Ne les écoutez pas! *etc.*

ALL THE GIRLS

Sir, don't listen to them! *etc.*

The soldiers keep the girls back. Carmen appears at the factory door, led by Don José and followed by two dragoons.

The factory-girls go out in a disorderly rush.

ZUNIGA

Voyons, brigadier … Maintenant que nous avons un peu de silence … qu'est-ce que vous avez trouvé là-dedans?

JOSÉ

J'ai trouvé trois cents femmes, hurlant, gesticulant. Il y en avait une qui avait sur la figure un X qu'on venait de lui marquer en deux coups de couteau … en face de la blessée …

On a glance from Carmen he stops.

ZUNIGA

Eh bien?

JOSÉ

J'ai vu mademoiselle …

ZUNIGA

Mademoiselle Carmencita?

JOSÉ

Oui, mon lieutenant.

ZUNIGA

Et qu'est-ce qu'elle disait, mademoiselle Carmencita?

JOSÉ

Elle ne disait rien, elle serrait les dents et roulait des yeux comme un caméleon.

ZUNIGA

Let's see, corporal … now that we've got a moment's silence … what did you find inside there?

JOSÉ

I found three hundred women, yelling and waving their arms about. There was one who had an X on her face that someone had just carved on her with two knife-slashes … Facing the wounded girl …

ZUNIGA

Well?

JOSÉ

I saw the señorita …

ZUNIGA

The señorita Carmencita?

JOSÉ

Yes, sir.

ZUNIGA

And what was she saying, the señorita Carmencita?

JOSÉ

She wasn't saying anything, she was gritting her teeth and rolling her eyes like a chameleon.

The lieutenant looks at Carmen; she, after a glance at Don José and a slight shrug of her shoulders, has become impassive again.

JOSÉ

J'ai prié mademoiselle de me suivre ...

JOSÉ

I asked the señorita to come with me ...

Carmen turns sharply and looks at José once more.

SCENE EIGHT
Song and Melodrama

DISC NO. 1/TRACK 9

Eh bien! ... vous avez entendu? ... Tra la la la Zuniga demands answers from Carmen, whose contemptuous defiance is dazzling. She sings nonsense in his face (00:09), daring him to cut her, burn her, whatever he wishes, but she will tell him nothing. There follows a section called a melodrama, in which Bizet underscored (as in a film score) (01:38) a section leading to spoken dialogue between Carmen and Don José, who is now charged with guarding her. The melodrama is often cut, though it appears in this recording to expand on what is a key moment in the relationship of Carmen and Don José.

ZUNIGA *(à Carmen)*

Eh bien! ... vous avez entendu? ... Avez-vous quelque chose à répondre? ... parlez, j'attends ...

ZUNIGA *(to Carmen)*

Well! ... you heard? ... Have you anything to answer? ... Speak, I'm waiting ...
Instead of replying, Carmen starts to sing.

Instead of replying, Carmen starts to sing.

CARMEN

Tra la la la, etc.
Coupe-moi, brûle-moi, je ne te dirai rien.
Tra la la la, etc.
Je brave tout, le feu, le fer et le ciel même.

CARMEN

Tra la la la, etc.
Cut me, burn me, I shall tell you nothing.
Tra la la la, etc.
I defy everything—fire, the sword and heaven itself.

ZUNIGA

Ce ne sont pas des chansons que je te demande, c'est une réponse.

ZUNIGA

It's not songs I'm asking you for, it's a reply.

CARMEN

Tra la la la, *etc.*
Mon secret je le garde et je le garde bien!
Tra la la la, *etc.*
J'en aime un autre et meurs en disant que je l'aime.

CARMEN

Tra la la la, *etc.*
I'm keeping my secret and keeping it close!
Tra la la la, *etc.*
I love another and I die in saying that I love him.

ZUNIGA

Ah! ah! nous le prenons sur ce ton-là … *à José* Ce qui est sûr, n'est-ce pas, c'est qu'il y eu des coups de couteau, et que c'est elle qui les a donnés …

ZUNIGA

Aha! So that's the attitude we're taking … to José What's certain, isn't it, is that there had been a knife attack and that it's she who made it …

At this moment five or six women on the right succeed in breaking the line of sentries and rush on to the stage shouting, "Yes, yes, it's her!" One of these women finds herself close by Carmen, who raises her hand and attempts to throw herself upon the woman. Don José stops Carmen. The soldiers haul the women off and this time force them back completely off the stage. A few sentinels remain in sight, guarding the approaches to the square.

ZUNIGA

Eh! vous avez la main leste décidément.
(Aux soldats) Trouvez-moi une corde.

ZUNIGA

Eh! decidedly you have a ready hand.
(to the soldiers) Find me a cord.

There is a moment of silence during which Carmen begins humming again in the most impertinent fashion as she watches the officer.

JOSE

Voilà, mon lieutenant.

JOSE

Here it is, sir.

ZUNIGA

Prenez et attachez-moi ces deux jolies mains.

ZUNIGA

Take this and tie those two pretty hands together for me.

Without offering the least resistance, Carmen smilingly holds out her two hands to Don José.

C'est dommage vraiment, car elle est gentille … si gentille que vous soyez, vous n'en irez pas moins faire un tour à la prison. Vous pourrez y chanter vos chansons de Bohémienne. Le porte-clefs vous dira ce qu'il en pense.

It's a shame, really, for she's pretty … But pretty as you may be, you're nonetheless going to take a stroll to the prison. You can sing your gypsy songs there. The turnkey'll tell you what he thinks of them.

Carmen's hands are bound and she is made to sit down on a stool in front of the guard-house. She remains motionless, her eyes cast down.

Je vais écrire l'ordre. *(à Don José)* C'est vous qui la conduirez …

I'm going to write out the order. (to Don José) It's you who will take her …

He goes out.

CARMEN

Où me conduirez-vous?

CARMEN

Where are you taking me?

DISC NO. 1/TRACK 10

JOSÉ

A la prison, ma pauvre enfant …

JOSÉ

To the jail, my poor child …

CARMEN

Hélas! que deviendrai-je? Seigneur officier, ayez pitié de moi … vous êtes si gentil. Laisse-moi m'échapper, je te donnerai un morceau de la bar lachi, une petite pierre qui te fera aimer de toutes les femmes.

CARMEN

Alas, what will become of me? Noble officer, take pity on me … You are so nice. Let me escape and I'll give you a piece of the bar lachi, a little stone which will make you loved by all women.

JOSÉ

moving away

Nous ne sommes pas ici pour dire des
balivernes ... Il faut aller à la prison. C'est
la consigne, et il n'y a pas de remède.

CARMEN

Camarade, mon ami, ne ferez-vous rien
pour une payse?

JOSÉ

Vous êtes Navarraise, vous?

CARMEN

Sans doute.

JOSÉ

Allons donc ... il n'y a pas un mot de vrai
... vos yeux seuls, votre bouche, votre teint
... tout vous dit Bohémienne ...

CARMEN

Bohémienne, tu crois?

JOSÉ

J'en suis sûr.

CARMEN

Au fait, je suis bien bonne de me donner
la peine de mentir ... Oui, je suis
Bohémienne, mais tu n'en feras pas moins
ce que je te demande ... tu le feras parce
que tu m'aimes ...

JOSÉ

We're not here to talk twaddle ... We must
go to the jail. Those are my instructions,
and there's no help for it.

CARMEN

Comrade of my heart, won't you do anything for a fellow-countrywoman?

JOSÉ

You're from Navarra, you?

CARMEN

Certainly.

JOSÉ

Come off it! ... There's not a word of
truth in it ... your eyes alone, your
mouth, your colouring ... everything pro-
claims you a gypsy ...

CARMEN

A gypsy, you think?

JOSÉ

I'm sure of it.

CARMEN

In fact, I am very simple to go to the trouble
of lying ... Yes, I'm a gypsy, but you'll
do what I want nonetheless ... You'll do it
because you love me ...

JOSÉ

Moi!

JOSÉ

I!

CARMEN

Eh! Oui, tu m'aimes. Cette fleur que tu as gardée—oh! Tu peux la jeter maintenant … cela n'y fera rien. La charme a opéré …

CARMEN

Ah yes, you love me. That flower you kept—oh, you can throw it away now … that makes no difference. The charm has worked …

JOSÉ *(avec colère)*

Ne me parle plus, tu entends, je te défends de me parler.

JOSÉ *(angrily)*

Don't talk to me any more, d'you hear, I forbid you to talk to me.

DISC NO. 1/TRACK 11

C'est très bien … Près des remparts de Séville (Seguedille) **Carmen has Don José in her sights, and, though her hands are bound, she sings this alluring aria to convince him into letting her escape. The aria begins as a seduction, insinuating and a little mysterious, but when Don José agrees to release her, Carmen repeats the melody with a bold, almost manic intensity (04:09), ending the aria with a shout of joy.**

CARMEN

C'est très bien, seigneur officier, c'est très bien. Vous me défendez de parler, je ne parlerai plus …

CARMEN

That's all right, officer sir, that's all right. You forbid me to talk, I'll not talk any more …

She looks at Don José who backs away.

Marilyn Horne as Carmen and James McCracken as Don José in Act 1.

SCENE NINE
Seguidilla and Duet

CARMEN

Près des remparts de Séville,
chez mon ami Lillas Pastia, j'irai danser la séguedille,
et boire du manzanilla.
J'irai chez mon ami Lillas Pastia!
Oui, mais toute seule on s'ennuie,
et les vrais plaisirs sont à deux.
Donc, pour me tenir compagnie,
j'emmènerai mon amoureux!
Mon amoureux … il est au diable
je l'ai mis à la porte hier.
Mon pauvre coeur très consolable,
mon coeur est libre comme l'air.
J'ai des galants à la douzaine,
mais ils ne sont pas à mon gré.
Voici la fin de la semaine,
qui veut m'aimer? Je l'aimerai
Qui veut mon âme? Elle est à prendre!

CARMEN

By the ramparts of Seville,
at my friend Lillas Pastia's place,
I'm going to dance the seguidilla
and drink manzanilla.
I'm going to my friend Lillas Pastia's!
Yes, but all alone one gets bored,
and real pleasures are for two.
So, to keep me company,
I shall take my lover!
My lover … he's gone to the devil
I showed him the door yesterday.
My poor heart, so consolable—
my heart is as free as air.
I have suitors by the dozen,
but they are not to my liking.
Here we are at week end;
Who wants to love me! I'll love him.
Who wants my heart? It's for the taking!

Vous arrivez au bon moment!
Je n'ai guère le temps d'attendre,
car avec mon nouvel amant …
Près des remparts de Séville, *etc.*

JOSÉ
Tais-toi! Je t'avais dit de ne pas me parler!

CARMEN
Je ne te parle pas,
je chante pour moi-même;
et je pense … il n'est pas défendu de
penser!
Je pense à certain officier,
qui m'aime, et qu'à mon tour,
oui, à mon tour je pourrais bien aimer!

JOSÉ
Carmen!

CARMEN
Mon officier n'est pas un capitaine,
pas même un lieutenant,
il n'est que brigadier;
mais c'est assez our une bohémienne,
et je daigne m'en contenter!

JOSÉ

untying Carmen's hands

Carmen, je suis comme un homme ivre,
se je cède, si je me livre,
ta promesse, tu la tiendras,
ah! si je t'aime, Carmen, tu m'aimeras?

You've come at the right moment!
I have hardly time to wait,
for with my new lover …
By the ramparts of Seville, *etc.*

JOSÉ
Stop! I told you not to talk to me!

CARMEN
I'm not talking to you,
I'm singing to myself;
and I'm thinking … it's not forbidden to
think!
I'm thinking about a certain officer
who loves me,
and whom in my turn I might really love!

JOSÉ
Carmen!

CARMEN
My officer's not a captain,
not even a lieutenant,
he's only a corporal;
but that's enough for a gypsy girl
and I'll deign to content myself with him!

JOSÉ

Carmen, I'm like a drunken man,
if I yield, if I give in,
you'll keep your promise?
Ah! If I love you, Carmen, you'll love me?

CARMEN	**CARMEN**
Oui …	Yes …
Nous danserons la séguedille	We'll dance the seguidilla
en buvant du manzanilla.	while we drink manzanilla.

JOSÉ	**JOSÉ**
Chez Lillas Pastia …	at Lillas Pastia's …
Tu le promets!	You promise!
Carmen …	Carmen …
Tu le promets!	You promise!

CARMEN	**CARMEN**
Ah! Près des remparts de Séville, *etc.*	Ah! By the ramparts of Seville, *etc.*

Her hands behind her, Carmen goes and re-seats herself on her stool.

Zuniga returns.

SCENE TEN

Finale

DISC NO. 1/TRACK 12

Furtive figures in the cellos play under Zuniga's calm instructions and Carmen's aside, giving us a "secret" peek into the escape plot as it is laid out. Carmen casually repeats snatches of her *Habanera* (00:39) as a flirtation and a warning that she is not to be trifled with.

ZUNIGA *(à José)*	**ZUNIGA** *(to José)*
Voici l'ordre; partez.	Here's the order; off you go now.
Et faites bonne garde.	And keep a good lookout.

CARMEN *(bas à José)*	**CARMEN** *(aside to José)*
En chemin je te pousserai,	On the way I shall push you,

je te pousserai aussi fort que je le pourrais …	I shall push you as hard as I can …
Laisse-toi renverser …	Let yourself fall over …
le reste me regarde.	The rest is up to me.

Carmen places herself between the two dragoons, with José at her side. The girls and others return onstage, kept back by the soldiers. Carmen crosses the stage, moving towards the bridge.

CARMEN

L'amour est enfant de bohéme,
il n'a jamais connu de loi.
Si tu ne m'aimes pas, je t'aime;
si je t'aime, prends garde à toi!

CARMEN

Love is a gypsy child,
he has never heard of law.
If you don't love me, I love you;
if I love you, look out for yourself!

Arriving at the foot of the bridge, Carmen pushes José, who falls. In the confusion Carmen takes to her heels. At the middle of the bridge she stops for a moment, sends her cord flying over the parapet of the bridge, and escapes, while the cigarette girls, with great shouts of laughter, surround Zuniga.

DISC NO. 1/TRACK 13

The orchestra plays a subtle and jaunty military tune which will later be sung by Don José. It is repeated by the basson for the second verse, creating a curiously bouncy, almost comical commentary.

ENTR'ACTE

Act 2

SCENE ELEVEN
Gypsy Song

The tavern of Lillas Pastia. Carmen, Mercédès, Frasquita, Lieutenant Zuniga, Moralès, and another lieutenant are there. A meal has just been finished and the table is in disorder. The officers and gypsy girls are smoking. Two gypsies are strumming guitars in a corner of the room; in the middle, two gypsy girls are singing. Carmen, seated, is watching them dance. An officer is talking to her quietly, but she pays him no attention whatsoever. Suddenly she gets up and begins to sing.

DISC NO. 1/TRACK 14

Les tringles des sistres tintaient (Chanson bohèmien) **The orchestra introduces the Gypsy Song with a hypnotic swirl in the flutes, accentuated on the off-beats by the harps. Carmen and her friends Frasquita and Mercédès sing and dance to the tune with a growing frenzy for the crowd at Lillas Pastia's. Carmen is at last seen and heard in her element, and the effect is mesmerizing—the beat of the last verse of the Gypsy Song (02:50) gets faster and faster until it drops from delirious exhaustion.**

CARMEN

Les tringles des sitres tintaient
avec un éclat métallique,
et sur cette étrange musique
les zingarellas se levaient.
Tambours de basque allaient leur train,
et les guitares forcenées
grinçaient sous des mains obsinées,
même chanson, même refrain.
Tralalalala …

CARMEN

The sistrums's* rods were jingling
with a metallic clatter,
and at this strange music
the zingarellas* leapt to their feet.
Tambourines were keeping time
and the frenzied guitars
ground away under persistent hands,
the same song, the same refrain.
Tralalalala …

* Sistrum: jingling instrument; rattle used by ancient nations.
* Zingarella: Zingara, Zingaro gypsy (It.).

During the refrain the gypsy girls dance, and Mercédès and Frasquita join Carmen in singing Tralalalala.

Les anneaux de cuivre et d'argent	Copper and silver rings
reluisaient sur les peaux bistrées;	glittered on dusky skins;
d'orange et de rouge zébrées	orange- and red-striped
les étouffes flottaient au vent.	dresses floated in the wind.
La danse au chant se mariait,	Dance and song became one—
d'abord indécise et timide,	at first timid and hesitant,
plus vive ensuite et plus rapide,	then livelier and faster
cela montait, montait, montait!	it grew and grew and grew!
Tralalalala …	Tralalalala …
Les bohémiens à tour de bras	The gypsy boys stormed away
de leurs instruments faisaient rage,	on their instruments with all their might,
et cet éblouissant tapage,	and this deafening uproar
ensorcelait les zingaras!	bewitched the zingaras!
Sous le rythme de la chanson,	Beneath the rhythm of the song,
ardentes, folles, enfiévrées,	passionate, wild, fired with excitement,
elles se laissaient, enivrées,	they let themselves be carried a way, intoxi-
emporter par le tourbillon!	cated, by the whirlwind!
Tralalalala …	Tralalalala …

At the conclusion of the dance Carmen sinks breathless on to a bench. Lillas Pastia begins to circulate among the officers. She looks worried.

DISC NO. 1/TRACK 15

ZUNIGA

Vous avez quelque chose à nous dire,
maître Lillas Pastia?

PASTIA

Mon Dieu, messieurs …

MORALÈS

Parle, voyons …

ZUNIGA

You've something to tell us, Master Lillas
Pastia?

PASTIA

My God, gentlemen …

MORALÈS

Speak, come now …

PASTIA

Il commence à se faire tard … et je suis, plus que personne, obligé d'observer les règlements.

MORALÈS

Cela veut dire que to nous mets à la porte! …

PASTIA

Oh! Non, messieurs les officiers, oh! non non … je vous fais seulement observer que mon auberge devrait être fermée depuis dix minutes …

ZUNIGA

Dieu sait ce qu'il s'y passe dans ton auberge, une fois qu'elle est fermée …

PASTIA

Oh! Mon lieutenant …

ZUNIGA

Enfin, nous avons encore, avant l'appel, le temps d'aller passer une heure au théâtre … vous y viendrez avec nous, n'est-ce pas, les belles?

Pastia signs to the gypsy girls to refuse.

FRASQUITA

Non, messieurs les officiers, non, nous restons ici, nous.

ZUNIGA

Comment, vous ne viendrez pas …

PASTIA

It's beginning to get late and I, more than anyone, am obliged to observe the regulations.

MORALÈS

That means that you're showing us the door!

PASTIA

Oh no. Officers, oh no! … I only remind you that my inn should have been closed ten minutes ago …

ZUNIGA

God knows what goes on in your inn after closing time …

PASTIA

Oh, sir! …

ZUNIGA

Anyway, we still have time before roll-call to pass an hour at the theatre … You'll come there with us, eh, girls?
Pastia signs to the gypsy girls to refuse.

FRASQUITA

No, officers, no, we're staying here, we are.

ZUNIGA

What, you're not coming?—

MERCÉDÈS

C'est impossible.

MORALÈS

Mercédès!

MERCÉDÈS

Je regrette …

MORALÈS

Frasquita!

FRASQUITA

Je suis désolée …

ZUNIGA

Mais toi, Carment, je suis bien sûr que tu ne refuseras pas …

CARMEN

C'est ce qui vous trompe, mon lieutenant … je refuse.

While the lieutenant is speaking to Carmen, two other lieutenants try to persuade Frasquita and Mercédès.

ZUNIGA

Tu m'en veux?

CARMEN

Pourquoi vous en voudrais-je?

ZUNIGA

Parce qu'il y a un mois, j'ai eu la cruauté de t'envoyer à la prison …

MERCÉDÈS

It's impossible.

MORALÈS

Mercédès!

MERCÉDÈS

Sorry …

MORALÈS

Frasquita!

FRASQUITA

Ever so sorry …

ZUNIGA

But you, Carmen, I'm quite sure you won't refuse …

CARMEN

That's where you're wrong, Lieutenant, I do refuse.

ZUNIGA

You've got a grudge against me?

CARMEN

Why should I have?

ZUNIGA

Because, a month ago, I was cruel enough to send you to prison …

CARMEN

as though she did not remember

A la prison … je ne me souviens pas d'être allée àla prison …

ZUNIGA

Je sais pardieu bien que tu n'y es pas allée … le brigadier qui était chargé de te conduire ayant jugé à propos de te laisser échapper … et de se faire dégrader et imprisonner pour cela …

CARMEN

serious

Dégrader et emprisonner?

ZUNIGA

Il a passé un mois en prison …

CARMEN

Mais il en est sorti?

ZUNIGA

Depuis hier seulement!

CARMEN

Tout est bien, puisqu'il en est sorti, tout est bien.

ZUNIGA

A la bonne heure, tu te consoles vite …

CARMEN

To prison? … I don't recall having gone to prison.

ZUNIGA

I know jolly well that you didn't go there … the corporal who had the job of taking you having opportunely decided to let you escape … and to get himself demoted and imprisoned for that …

CARMEN

Demoted and imprisoned?

ZUNIGA

He's spent a month in prison …

CARMEN

But he's out now?

ZUNIGA

Only since yesterday!

CARMEN

Everything's all right then, since he is out, everything's all right.

ZUNIGA

Well well, you console yourself quickly …

CARMEN	CARMEN
Si vous m'en croyez, vous ferez comme moi, vous voulez nous emmener, nous ne voulons pas vous suivre ... vous vous consolerez ...	If you take my advice you'll do like me; you want to take us out, we don't want to come with you ... you will console yourselves ...

MORALÈS	MORALÈS
Il faudra bien.	We'll have to.

The scene is interrupted by a chorus sung in the wings.

SCENE TWELVE
Chorus and Ensemble

DISC NO. 1/TRACK 16

The chorus is heard off-stage as the others inside continue their conversation. Even before we meet Escamillo, the chorus and the heavy brass in the orchestra tell us of his warrior character.

CHOEUR	CHORUS
Vivat! vivat le toréro!	Hurrah! Hurrah for the torero!
Vivat! vivat Escamillo! *etc.*	Hurrah! Hurrah for Escamillo! *etc.*

The dialogue continues during the singing of the above Chorus.

ZUNIGA	ZUNIGA
Qu'est-ce que c'est que ça?	What's all that?

MERCÉDÈS	MERCÉDÈS
Une promenade aux flambeaux ...	A torchlight procession ...

FRASQUITA

C'est Escamillo … un torero qui s'est fait remarquer aux dernières courses de Grenade.

MORALÈS

Pardieu, il faut le faire venir … nous boirons en son honneur!

ZUNIGA

C'est cela, je vais l'inviter.

He goes over to the window.

Monsieur le toréro … voulez-vous faire l'amitié de monter ici? Vous y trouverez des gens qui aiment fort tous ceux qui, comme vous ont de l'adresse et du courage.

CHOEUR

Vivat! vivat le toréro!
Vivat! vivat Escamillo! *etc.*

Enter Escamillo.

ZUNIGA

Nous vous remercions d'avoir accepté notre invitation; nous n'avons pas voulu vous laisser passer sans boire avec vous au grand art de la tauromachie.

ESCAMILLO

Messieurs les officiers, je vous remercie.

FRASQUITA

It's Escamillo … a bullfighter who distinguished himself at the last Granada meetings.

MORALÈS

By jove, we must get him up here … we'll drink in his honour!

ZUNIGA

That's it, I'll invite him.

Señor torero, will you do us the kindness to step up here? You'll find chaps who are very fond of all those, like yourself, who have skill and courage …

CHORUS

Hurrah! Hurrah for the torero!
Hurrah! Hurrah for Escamillo! *etc.*

ZUNIGA

We thank you for having accepted our invitation; we didn't want to let you go by without drinking with you to the great art of tauromachy.

ESCAMILLO

Gentlemen, I thank you.

DISC NO. 1/TRACK 17

Votre toast, je peux vous le rendre (Toreador Song) One of the most famous arias in all of opera, Escamillo's Toreador Song is a celebration of the swaggering macho tradition. The arresting verses are in a minor key. In them, the toreador describes his exploits and their dangers. However, the refrain ("Toréador, en garde …") is in the major. This proud, striding melody (01:19) becomes Escamillo's identity as he sings of the love that awaits him when his trials are over.

ESCAMILLO

Votre toast, je peux vous le rendre,
señors, car avec les soldats,
oui, les toréros peuvent s'entendre,
pour plaisirs ils ont les combats!
Le cirque est plein, c'est jour de fête,
le cirque est plein du haut en bas.
Les spectateurs perdant la tête,
les spectateurs s'interpellent à grand fracas!
Apostrophes, cris et tapage
poussés jusques à la fureur!
Car c'est la fête du courage!
C'est la fête des gens de coeur!
Allons! en garde! ah!
Toréador, en garde!
Et songe bien, oui, songe en combattant,
qu'un oeil noir te regarde
et que l'amour t'attend!
Toréador, l'amour t'attend!

ESCAMILLO

I can return your toast,
gentlemen, for soldiers—
yes—and bullfighters understand each
other; fighting is their game!
The ring is packed, it's a holiday,
the ring is full from top to bottom.
The spectators, losing their wits,
yell at each other at the tops of their voices!
Exclamations, cries and uproar
carried to the pitch of fury!
For this is the fiesta of courage,
this is the fiesta of the stouthearted!
Let's go! On guard! Ah!
Toreador, on guard!
And remember, yes, remember as you fight
that two dark eyes are watching you,
that love awaits you!
Toreador, love awaits you!

TOUT LE MONDE

Toréador, en garde! *etc.*

CHORUS

Toreador, on guard! *etc.*

Carmen refills Escamillo's glass.

ESCAMILLO

Tout d'un coup, on fait silence,

on fait silence, ah! que se passe-t-il?

Plus de cris, c'est l'instant!

Le taureau s'élance

en bondissant hors du toril!

Il s'élance! Il entre, il frappe!

Un cheval roule, entraînant un picador!

"Ah! bravo Toro!" hurle la foule;

le taureau va, il vient,

il vient et frappe encore!

En secouant ses banderilles,

plein de fureur, il court!

Le cirque est plein de sang!

On se sauve, on franchit les grilles.

C'est ton tour maintenant!

Allons! en garde! ah!

Toréador, en garde! *etc.*

TOUT LE MONDE

Toréador, en garde! etc.

.... l'amour t'attend!

ESCAMILLO

Suddenly everyone falls silent;

ah—what's happening?

No more shouts, this is the moment!

The bull comes bounding

out of the toril!

He charges, comes in, strikes!

A horse rolls over, dragging down a pica-

dor! "Ah! Bravo bull!" roars the crowd;

the bull turns, comes back.

Comes back and strikes again!

Shaking his banderillas,

maddened with rage, he runs about!

The ring is covered with blood!

Men jump clear, leap the barriers.

It's your turn now!

Let's go! On guard! Ah!

Toreador, on guard! *etc.*

CHORUS

Toreador, on guard! etc.

… love awaits you!

SCENE THIRTEEN B
Toreador's song

FRASQUITA

L'Amour!

ESCAMILLO

L'Amour!

FRASQUITA

Love!

ESCAMILLO

Love!

MERCÉDÈS	**MERCÉDÈS**
L'Amour!	Love!
ESCAMILLO	**ESCAMILLO**
L'Amour!	Love!
CARMEN	**CARMEN**
L'Amour!	Love!
ALL	**ALL**
Toréador! Toréador! L'amour t'attend!	Toreador, Toreador, love awaits you!

They drink and exchange handshakes with the toreador.

DISC NO. 1/TRACK 18

Carmen's initial flirtation is, rather surprisingly, all accomplished in dialogue rather than music. Escamillo's exit from the stage, however, is a swaggering orchestral restatement (00:58) of his Toreador Song.

PASTIA	**PASTIA**
Messieurs les officiers, je vous en prie.	Officers, sirs, I beg you.
ZUNIGA	**ZUNIGA**
C'est bien, c'est bien, nous partons.	All right, all right, we're going.

The officers start to get ready to leave. Escamillo finds himself beside Carmen.

ESCAMILLO	**ESCAMILLO**
Dis-moi ton nom, et la première fois que je frapperai le taureau, ce sera ton nom que je prononcerai.	Tell me your name, and the first time I kill a bull it will be your name that I utter.
CARMEN	**CARMEN**
Je m'appelle la Carmencita.	I'm called Carmencita.

ESCAMILLO

La Carmencita?

CARMEN

Carmen, la Carmencita, comme tu voudras.

ESCAMILLO

Eh bien! Carmen ou la Carmencita, si je m'avisais de t'aimer et d'être aimé de toi, qu'est-ce tu me répondrais?

CARMEN

Je répondrais que tu peux m'aimer tout à ton aise mais que quant à être aimé de moi pour le moment, il n'y faut pas songer!

ESCAMILLO

J'attendrai alors et me contenterai d'espérer …

CARMEN

Il n'est pas défendu d'attendre et il est toujours agréable d'espérer.

ZUNIGA

quietly to Carmen

Ecoute-moi, Carmen, puisque tu ne veux pas venir avec nous, c'est moi qui dans une heure reviendrai ici …

CARMEN

Je ne vous conseille pas de revenir…

ESCAMILLO

Carmencita?

CARMEN

Carmen, Carmencita, as you like.

ESCAMILLO

Well then! Carmen or Carmencita, if I took it into my head to love you and be loved by you, what would you answer?

CARMEN

I should answer that you can love me just as you please, but as for being loved by me just at present, you mustn't think of it!

ESCAMILLO

Then I'll wait, and content myself with hoping …

CARMEN

It's not forbidden to wait, and it's always pleasant to hope.

ZUNIGA

Listen to me, Carmen. Since you won't come with us, it's I who'll come back here in an hour …

CARMEN

I don't advise you to come back …

ZUNIGA

quietly to Carmen

Je reviendrai tout le même.

Nous partons avec vous, torero, et nous
nous joindrons au cortège qui vous
accompagne.

ZUNIGA

I'll come back all the same.

We'll leave with you, torero, and tack
ourselves on to the procession that accompa-
nies you.

Everybody goes out except Carmen, Frasquita, Mercédès, and Lillas Pastia.

DISC NO. 1/TRACK 19

FRASQUITA *(à Pastia)*
Pourquoi étas-tu si pressé de les fair partir?

FRASQUITA *(to Pastia)*
Why were you so eager to send them away?

PASTIA
Le Dancaïre et Le Remendado viennent
d'arriver …

PASTIA
Dancaïro and Remendado have just
arrived …

PASTIA

opening a door and gesturing as he calls out

Les voici …

PASTIA

Here they are …

Enter Dancaïro and Remendado. Pastia closes the doors, puts up the shutters, etc., etc.

FRASQUITA
Eh bien, les nouvelles?

FRASQUITA
Well, the news?

LE DANCAÏRE
Pas trop mauvaises, les nouvelles; nous
arrivons de Gibraltar.

EL DANCAÏRO
Not too bad, the news. We've just come
from Gibraltar.

LE REMENDADO

Jolie ville, Gibraltar! … on y voit des
Anglais, beaucoup d'Anglais, de jolis
hommes les Anglais, un peu froids, mais
distingués.

LE DANCAÏRE

Remendado! …

LE REMENDADO

Patron.

LE DANCAÏRE

Taisez-vous. Nous avons arrangé l'embar-
quement de marchandises anglaises. Nous
irons les attendre près de la côte, nous en
cacherons une partie dans la montagne et
nous ferons passer le reste. Tous nos cama-
rades ont été prévenus … mais c'est de
vous trois surtout ue nous avons besoin
…vous allez partir avec nous.

CARMEN (riant)

Pourquoi faire? Pour vous aider à porter
des ballots?

LE REMENDADO

Oh! Non… faire porter des ballots à des
dames … ça ne serait pas distingué.

LE DANCAÏRE (menaçant)

Remendado?

LE REMENDADO

Oui, patron.

EL REMENDADO

Nice town, Gibraltar! … you see the
English there, lots of English, nice chaps
the English, a trifle cold, but gentlemanly.

EL DANCAÏRO

Remendado! …

EL REMENDADO

Boss.

EL DANCAÏRO

Shut up. We are arranged to take on board
some English goods. We're going to wait
for it near the coast. We'll hide some of the
stuff up the mountain and run the rest. All
our comrades have been warned … but it's
you three we need principally … you'll
leave with us.

CARMEN (laughing)

What for? To help you carry the bales?

EL REMENDADO

Oh no!—make the ladies carry the bales …
that wouldn't be at all the thing.

EL DANCAÏRO (threateningly)

Remendado?

EL REMENDADO

Yes, boss.

LE DANCAÏRE

Nous ne vous ferons pas porter de ballots, mais nous avons besoin de vous pour autre chose.

EL DANCAÏRO

We're not going to make you carry any bales, but we do need you for something else.

Mary Garden in the role of Carmen.

SCENE FOURTEEN
Quintet

DISC NO. 1/TRACK 20

Nous avons en tête une affaire (Quintet) The quintet is a fleet-footed miracle that, like Micaëla's scene with Don José in Act I, comes along like a cooling breeze to relieve all the erotic heat. It introduces outright comedy in the persons of the smugglers Dancaïro and Remendado who, with Frasquita and Mercédès, want Carmen to help them with a shipment of contraband. The men are bent on having the women flirt with the guards so the smugglers can slip past customs at the border. The heightened musical energy (04:02) of the quintet is an imaginative depiction of five sociopaths plotting their next bit of mischief. The subsequent dialogue (05:10) is spoken over the approaching song of Don José, which is a more heroic version of the military tune played for the entr'acte.

LE DANCAÏRE

Nous avons en tête une affaire.

EL DANCAÏRO

We have a scheme in mind.

MERCÉDÈS ET FRASQUITA

Est-elle bonne, dites-nous?

MERCÉDÈS AND FRASQUITA

Tell us, is it good?

LE DANCAÏRE ET LE REMENDADO

Elle est admirable, ma chère;
mais nous avons besoin de vous.

EL DANCAÏRO AND EL REMENDADO

It's admirable, my dear;
but we require your services.

TOUS LE CINQ

De nous? *etc.*
De vous! *etc.*

QUINTET

Ours? *etc.*
Yours! *etc.*

LES DEUX HOMMES

Car nous l'avouons humblement,
et fort respectueusement;
quand il s'agit de tromperie,
de duperie, de volerie,
il est toujous bon, sur ma foi,

THE TWO MEN

For we humbly
and most respectfully acknowledge
when it's a question of trickery
of deception, of thieving,
it's always good, I swear,

d'avoir les femmes avec soi.
Et sans elles,
mes toutes belles,
on ne fait jamais rien
de bien!

LES TROIS FEMMES
Quoi! sans nous jamais rien
de bien?

LES DEUX HOMMES
N'êtes-vous pas de cet avis?

LES TROIS FEMMES
Si fait, je suis
de cet avis.
Si fait, vraiment je suis.

TOUS LES CINQ
Quand il s'agit de tromperie, *etc.*

LE DANCAÏRE
C'est dit alors; vous partirez?

FRASQUITA ET MERCÉDÈS
Quand vous voudrez.

LE DANCAÏRE
Mais tout de suite.

CARMEN
Ah! permettez!!
S'il vous plait de partir, partez,
mais je ne suis pas du voyage.
Je ne pars pas, je ne pars pas!

to have women around.
And without them,
my lovelies,
no one ever does
any good!

THE THREE GIRLS
What? Without us no one does
any good?

THE TWO MEN
Isn't that your opinion?

GIRLS
Indeed, that's
my opinion.
Yes indeed, really it is.

QUINTET
When it's a question of trickery, *etc.*

EL DANCAÏRO
It's settled then; you'll go?

FRASQUITA AND MERCÉDÈS
Whenever you like.

EL DANCAÏRO
Why, straight away.

CARMEN
Ah! just a moment!
If you want to go, go;
but I'm not in on this trip.
I won't go! I won't go!

LES DEUX HOMMES

Carmen, mon amour, tu viendras—

CARMEN

Je ne pars pas; je ne pars pas!

LES DEUX HOMMES

Et tu n'auras pas le courage
de nous laisser dans l'embarras.

FRASQUITA ET MERCÉDÈS

Ah! ma Carmen, tu viendras.

CARMEN

Je ne pars pas, *etc.*

LE DANCAÏRE

Mais, au moins la raison, Carmen,
tu la diras.

TOUS LES QUATRE

La raison, la raison!

CARMEN

Je la dirai certainement.

TOUS LES QUATRE

Voyons! Voyons!

CARMEN

La raison, c'est qu'en ce moment …

TOUS LES QUATRE

Eh bien? Eh bien?

THE MEN

Carmen, my love, you will come—

CARMEN

I won't go! I won't go!

THE MEN

And you won't have the heart
to leave us in the lurch.

FRASQUITA AND MERCÉDÈS

Ah! My Carmen, you will come.

CARMEN

I won't go! *etc.*

EL DANCAÏRO

But the reason, Carmen,
at least you'll tell us the reason.

QUARTET

The reason, the reason!

CARMEN

Certainly I'll give it.

QUARTET

Let's have it! Let's have it!

CARMEN

The reason is that at this moment …

QUARTET

Well? Well?

CARMEN

Je suis amoureuse!

LES DEUX HOMMES *(stupéfaits)*

Qu'a-t-elle dit?

LES DEUX FEMMES

Elle dit qu'elle est amoureuse!

TOUS LES QUATRE

Amoureuse!

CARMEN

Oui, amoureuse!

LE DANCAÏRE

Voyons, Carmen, sois sérieuse!

CARMEN

Amoureuse à perdre l'esprit!

LES DEUX HOMMES

La chose, certes, nous étonne,

mais ce n'est pas le premier jour

où vous aurez su, ma mignonne,

faire marcher de front le devoir et l'amour.

CARMEN

Mes amis, je serais fort aise

de partir avec vous ce soir;

mais cette fois ne vous déplaise,

il faudra que l'amour passe avant le devoir.

LE DANCAÏRE

Ce n'est pas là ton dernier mot?

CARMEN

I'm in love!

THE MEN *(astonished)*

What did she say?

THE GIRLS

She says she's in love!

QUARTET

In love!

CARMEN

Yes, in love!

EL DANCAÏRO

See here, Carmen, be serious!

CARMEN

Head over heels in love!

THE MEN

This is certainly astonishing,

but it's not the first time,

my pet, that you've been able

to combine love and duty.

CARMEN

My friends, I'd be most happy

to go with you this evening;

but this time—don't be annoyed—

love must come before duty.

EL DANCAÏRO

That's not your final word?

CARMEN

Absolument!

LE REMENDADO

Il faut que tu te laisses attendrir.

TOUS LES QUATRE

Il faut venir, Carmen, il faut venir!

Pour notre affaire,

c'est nécessaire,

car entre nous …

CARMEN

Quant à cela, je l'admets avec vous …

RPRISE GÉNÉRALE

Quand il s'agit de tromperie, etc.

LE DANCAÏRE

En voilà assez; je t'ai dit qu'il faillait venir

et tu viendras … je suis le chef.

CARMEN

Comment dis-tu ça?

LE DANCAÏRE

Je te dis que je suis le chef.

CARMEN

Et tu crois que je t'obéirai?

LE DANCAÏRE *(furieux)*

Carmen! …

CARMEN

Absolutely!

EL REMENDADO

You must relent.

QUARTET

You must come, Carmen, you must come!

It's necessary

for our scheme,

for between ourselves …

CARMEN

As to that, I admit with you that …

QUINTET *(reprise)*

When it's a question of trickery, etc.

EL DANCAÏRO

Enough of that; I told you you must come,

and you will come … I am the leader.

CARMEN

What's that you say?

EL DANCAÏRO

I tell you I'm the leader.

CARMEN

And you think I'll obey you?

EL DANCAÏRO *(furious)*

Carmen! …

LE REMENDADO

throwing himself between Dancaïro and Carmen

Je vous en prie … des personnes si distin-
guées.

LE DANCAÏRE

Amoureuse … ce n'est pas une raison, cela.

CARMEN

Partez sans moi … j'irai vous rejoindre
demain, mais pour ce soir je reste.

FRASQUITA

Je ne t'ai jamais vue comme cela; que
attends-tu donc?

CARMEN

Un pauvre diable du soldat qui m'a rendu
service …

MERCÉDÈS

Ce soldat qui était en prison?

CARMEN

Oui.

LE DANCAÏRE

Je parierais qu'il ne viendra pas.

CARMEN

Ne parie pas, tu perdrais …

José's voice is heard in the distance.

EL REMENDADO

I beg you, such genteel persons.

EL DANCAÏRO

In love … that's not a reason.

CARMEN

Leave without me. I'll come and join you
tomorrow, but for this evening I'm staying.

FRASQUITA

I've never seen you like this. Who are you
expecting?

CARMEN

A poor devil of a soldier who did me a
service …

MERCÉDÈS

That soldier who was in prison?

CARMEN

Yes.

EL DANCAÏRO

I'd bet you he won't come.

CARMEN

Don't bet, you would lose …

SCENE FIFTEEN
Song

JOSÉ

in the far distance

Halte là!
Qui va là?
Dragon d'Alcala!
Où t'en vas-tu par là,
Dragon d'Alcala?—
Moi, je m'en vais faire
mordre la poussière
à mon adversaire.—
S'il en est ainsi,
passez, mon ami.
Affaire d'honneur,
affaire de coeur;
pour nous tout est là
Dragons d'Alcala!

JOSÉ

Halt!
Who goes there?
Dragoon of Alcala!
Where are you going there,
Dragoon of Alcala?—
Me, I'm going to make
my rival
bite the dust.—
If that's the case,
pass, my friend.
An affair of honour,
an affair of the heart—
that explains everything for us
Dragoons of Alcala!

There is no break in the music. Carmen, Dancaïro, Remendado, Mercédès, and Frasquita watch the arrival of José through the half-open shutters.

MERCÉDÈS
C'est un dragon, ma foi.

MERCÉDÈS
Faith, it's a dragoon.

FRASQUITA
Un beau dragon

FRASQUITA
A handsome dragoon.

LE DANCAÏRE *(à Carmen)*
Eh bien, Carmen, puisque tu ne veux venir
que demain, sais-tu au moins ce que tu
devrais faire?

EL DANCAÏRO *(to Carmen)*
Well, Carmen, since you won't come until
tomorrow, d'you know at least what you
ought to do?

CARMEN

Qu'est-ce que je devrais faire?

LE DANCAÏRE

Tu devrais décider ton dragon à venir avec toi et à se joindre à nous.

CARMEN

Ah! … si cela se pouvait! … Mais il n'y faut pas penser … ce sont des bêtises … il est trop niais.

LE DANCAÏRE

Pourquoi l'aimes-tu puisque tu en conviens toi-même?

CARMEN

Parce qu'il est joli garçon donc et qu'il me plaît.

LE REMENDADO *(avec fatuité)*

Le patron ne comprend pas ça, lui … qu'il suffise d'être joli garçon pour plaire aux femmes …

LE DANCAÏRE

Attends un peu, toi, attends un peu …

Remendado makes his escape and goes out. Dancaïro pursues him and goes out in his turn, dragging along Mercédès and Frasquita who are trying to calm him down.

JOSÉ

Halte là!

Qui va là?

Dragon d'Alcala!

CARMEN

What is it I ought to do?

EL DANCAÏRO

You ought to persuade your dragoon to come with you and join us.

CARMEN

Ah, if that were possible! … But you mustn't think of it … it's nonsense … he's too simple.

EL DANCAÏRO

Why do you love him, since you yourself admit it?

CARMEN

Because he's a nice boy and he pleases me.

EL REMENDADO *(fatuously)*

The boss, he doesn't understand that … that it's enough to be a nice boy in order to please the women …

EL DANCAÏRO

Wait a moment, you, wait a moment …

JOSÉ

Halt!

Who goes there?

Dragoon of Alcala!

Où t'en vas-tu par là,	Where are you going there,
Dragon d'Alcala?—	Dragoon of Alcala?—
Exact et fidèle,	Punctual and faithful,
je vais où m'appelle	I go where the love
l'amour de ma belle!—	of my fair lady calls me!—
S'il en est ainsi,	If that's the case,
passez, mon ami.	pass, friend.
Affaire d'honneur,	An affair of honour,
affaire de coeur,	an affair of the heart,
pour nous tout est là,	that explains everything for us
Dragons d'Alcala!	Dragoons of Alcala!

Don José enters.

CARMEN	**CARMEN**
Enfin … te voilà … C'est bien heureux!	At last … so there you are … this is a fine thing!
JOSÉ	**JOSÉ**
Il y a deux heures seulement que je suis	It's only two hours since I came out of
sorti de prison.	prison.
CARMEN	**CARMEN**
Qui t'empêchait de sortir plus tôt? Je	What prevented you from getting out sooner?
t'avais envoyé une lime et une pièce d'or.	I had sent you a file and a gold coin.
JOSÉ	**JOSÉ**
Que veux-tu? J'ai encore mon honneur de	What d'you expect? I still have my soldier's
soldat, et déserter me semblerait un grand	honour, and to desert would seem to be a
crime … Oh! Je ne t'en suis pas moins	great crime … Oh, I'm none the less grate-
reconnaissant. La lime me servira pour	ful to you. The file will be useful to me for
affiler ma lance et je l'ai gardé comme	sharpening my lance and I've kept it as a
souvenir de toi.	memento of you.

holding out the gold coin to her

Quant a l'argent …	As for the money …

CARMEN

Tiens, il l'a gardé!

shouting and hammering

Holà! … Lillas Pastia, holà!

enter Pastia

CARMEN

tossing him the coin

Apporte-nous du Manzanilla … apporte-nous de tout ce que tu as, de tout …

PASTIA

Tout de suite, mademoiselle Carmencita.

He goes out.

CARMEN *(à Don José)*

Tu regrettes d t'être fait mettre en prison pour mes beaux yeux?

JOSÉ

Non. On m'a mis en prison, on m'a ôté mon grade, mais ça m'est égal.

CARMEN

Parce que tu m'aimes?

JOSÉ

Oui, parce que je t'aime, parce que je t'adore.

CARMEN

Hullo, he's kept it!

Hi there! … Lillas Pastia, hi!

CARMEN

Bring us some Manzanilla … bring us everything you have, everything, the lot …

PASTIA

At once, señorita Carmencita.

CARMEN *(to Don José)*

You regret having been put in prison for the sake of my lovely eyes?

JOSÉ

No. They put me in prison, they stripped me of my rank, but it's all one to me.

CARMEN

Because you love me?

JOSÉ

Yes, because I love you, because I adore you.

CARMEN

Ton lieutenant était ici tour à l'heure, avec d'autres officiers, ils nous ont fait danser.

CARMEN

Your lieutenant was here just now with some other officers. They made us dance.

JOSÉ

Tu as dansé?

JOSÉ

You danced?

CARMEN

Oui; et ton lieutenant s'est permis de me dire qu'il m'adorait …

CARMEN

Yes; and your lieutenant allowed himself to tell me that he adored me …

JOSÉ

Carmen!

JOSÉ

Carmen!

CARMEN

Qu'est-ce que tu as? … Est-ce que tu serais jaloux, par hasard?

CARMEN

What's the matter with you? … Would you be jealous, by any chance?

Shirley Verrett (b. 1931) made her Metropolitan Opera debut in the title role of Carmen.

JOSÉ

Mais certainement, je suis jaloux …

CARMEN

Eh bien, si tu le veux, je danserai pour toi
maintenant, pour toi seul.

JOSÉ

Ah! que je t'aime, Carmen, que je t'aime!

CARMEN

Je l'espère bien.

JOSÉ

Why, certainly I'm jealous …

CARMEN

Well then, if you want me to, I'll dance for
you now, for you alone.

JOSÉ

Ah, how I love you, Carmen, how I love you!

CARMEN

So I should hope.

SCENE SIXTEEN
Duet

DISC NO. 2/TRACK 1

Je vais danser en votre honneur **Don José arrives, fresh from his stint in prison, and Carmen greets
him with some teasing and as a special treat she dances for him alone (00:37) in a way that suggests a tempestuous night of love is ahead for them. But Bizet brilliantly dramatizes the central
conflict of the story in a few well-chosen strokes when he has Don José hear the reveille (01:13).
Carmen's explosive anger (02:39) when he tells her he must leave has an unsettling effect on
Don José, whose psychotic reaction in the end is underlined by the return of the fate motive,
heard in the opera's prelude.**

CARMEN

Je vais danser en votre honneur,
et vous verrez, seigneur,
comment je sais moi-même accompagner
ma danse!
Mettez-vous là, Don José, je commence!

CARMEN

I am going to dance in your honour,
and you will see, my lord,
how I am able to accompany
my dance!
Sit down there, Don José, I'll begin!

She makes José sit down in a corner, and starts to dance, humming and accompanying herself with her castanets. José is entranced. Bugles are heard in the distance sounding Retreat. José cocks an ear. He comes over to Carmen and compels her to stop.

JOSÉ

Attendez, Carmen, rien qu'un moment,
arrêtte!

CARMEN

Et pour quoi, s'il te plaît?

JOSÉ

Il me semble, là-bas …
oui, ce sont nos clairons que sonnent la
retraite!
Ne les entends-tu pas?

CARMEN

Bravo! Bravo! J'avais beau faire; il est
mélancholique de danser sans orchestre.
Et vive la musique
qui nous tombe du ciel!

JOSÉ

Wait, Carmen, only for a moment,
stop!

CARMEN

And why, if you please?

JOSÉ

I think, over there …
yes, those are our bugles sounding
Retreat!
Can't you hear them?

CARMEN

Bravo! Bravo! I was trying in vain; it's dismal
dancing without an orchestra.
And long live music
that drops on us out of the skies!

She resumes her song. The bugles sound nearer, pass beneath the windows of the inn, then fade in the distance. José makes a new effort to tear himself from his contemplation of Carmen. He seizes her arm and compels her to stop once more.

JOSÉ

Tu ne m'as pas compris, Carmen, c'est la
retraite;
il faut que moi, je rentre au quartier pour
l'appel

CARMEN

Au quartier! Pour l'appel!

JOSÉ

You didn't understand me, Carmen, it's
Retreat;
I've got to get back to quarters
for roll-call.

CARMEN

To quarters! For roll-call!

Ah! j'étais vraiment trop bête!	Ah! Really I was too stupid!
Je me mettais en quartre	I went out of my way
et je faisais des frais,	and took the trouble,
oui, je faisais des frais	yes, I took the trouble
pour amuser monsieur!	to entertain the gentleman!
Je chantais! Je dansais!	I sang! I danced!
Je crois, Dieu me pardonne,	I believe, God forgive me,
qu'un peu plus, je l'aimais!	I almost fell in love!
Taratata!	Taratata!
C'est le clarion qui sonne!	It's the bugle sounding!
Taratata!	Taratata!
Il part! il est parti!	He's off! He's gone!
Va-t'en donc, canari!	Go on then, canary!*

angrily throwing his cap at him

Tiens; prends ton shako,	Here! Take your shako,
ton sabre, ta giberne;	your sword, your bandolier;
et va-t'en, mon garçon, va-t'en!	and clear off, my son, clear off!
Retourne à ta caserne!	Clear off back to your barracks!

JOSÉ

C'est mal à toi, Carmen, de te moquer de moi! Je souffre de partir, car jamais, jamais femme, jamais femme avant toi, aussi profoundemént n'avait troublé mon âme!

JOSÉ

It's cruel of you, Carmen, to make fun of me! It pains me to go, for never, never has a woman, never before you has any woman so deeply stirred my heart!

CARMEN

"Taratata, mon Dieu! C'est la retraite! Taratata, je vais être en retard!" Il court, il perd la tête, et voilà son amour!

CARMEN

"Taratata, my God! It's the Retreat! Taratata, I'm going to be late!" He loses his wits, he rushes off, and that's his love!

* a reference to the yellow tunic of a Spanish dragoon.

JOSÉ	JOSÉ
Ainsi, tu ne crois pas à mon amour?	So you don't believe in my love?

CARMEN	CARMEN
Mais non!	Of course not!

JOSÉ	JOSÉ
Eh bien! tu m'entendras!	Very well! You shall listen to me!

CARMEN	CARMEN
Je ne veux rien entendre!	I won't listen to anything!

JOSÉ	JOSÉ
Tu m'entendras!	You shall hear me!

CARMEN	CARMEN
Tu vas te faire attendre!	You're going to be late!

JOSÉ	JOSÉ
Tu m'entendras! Carmen!	You shall hear me! Carmen!

CARMEN	CARMEN
Non! non! non! non!	No! No! No! No!

JOSÉ	JOSÉ
Oui, tu m'entendras!	Yes, you shall hear me!
Je le veux! Carmen,	I insist! Carmen,
tu m'entendras!	you shall hear me!

He reaches inside his tunic and takes out the acacia flower Carmen threw him in Act One.

DISC NO. 2/TRACK 2

La fleur que tu m'avais jetée (Flower Song) **The Flower Song is the tenor's big solo moment in Carmen, a beautiful aria that challenges the singer to deliver it with passion and, at the same time, a kind of neurotic tenderness. It is one of those arias with such beautiful surfaces that one does** not have to look beneath them to appreciate it. Yet it is a disturbing moment in the context of the opera—a quality captured in Jon Vickers's performance on this recording—that ends with passionate declaration that rises (03:19) to an eerily soft high B-flat.

La fleur que tu m'avais jetée,	The flower that you threw to me
dans ma prison m'était restée.	stayed with me in my prison.
Flétrie et sèche, cette fleur	Withered and dried up, that flower
gardait toujours sa douce odeur;	always kept its sweet perfume;
et pendant des heures entières,	and for hours at a time,
sur mes yeux, fermant mes paupières,	with my eyes closed,
de cette odeur je m'enivrais	I became drunk with its smell
et dans la nuit je te voyais!	and in the night I used to see you!
Je me prenais à te maudire,	I took to cursing you,
à te détester, à me dire	detesting you, asking myself
Pourquoi faut-it que le destin,	why did destiny
l'ait mise là sur mon chemin?	have to throw her across my path?
Puis je m'accusais de blasphème,	Then I accused myself of blasphemy,
et je ne sentais en moi-même,	and felt within myself,
je ne sentais qu'un seul désir,	I felt but one desire,
un seul désir, un seul espoir	one desire, one hope
te revoir, ô Carmen, oui, te revoir!	to see you again, Carmen, to see you again!
Car tu n'avais eu qu'à paraître,	For you had only to appear,
qu'à jeter un regard sur moi,	only to throw a glance my way,
pour t'emparer de tour mon être,	to take possession of my whole being,
ô ma Carmen!	O my Carmen,
et j'étais une chose à toi!	and I was your chattel!
Carmen, je t'aime!	Carmen, I love you!

DISC NO. 2/TRACK 3

Non! tu ne maimes pas! Carmen sees the potential for exploiting Don José's vulnerability and, in a rhythmically seductive phrase beginning with the words "Là-bas, là-bas …" (00:19), she insists (much as she insisted in the Seguedille) that he join her and her smuggler friends.

CARMEN	**CARMEN**
Non, tu ne m'aimes pas!	No, you don't love me!

JOSÉ

Que dis-tu?

CARMEN

Non, tu ne m'aimes pas,
non! Car si tu m'aimais,
là-bas, là-bas,
tu me suivrais.

JOSÉ

Carmen!

CARMEN

Oui!—
Là-bas, là-bas, dans la montagne,

JOSÉ

Carmen!

CARMEN

là-bas, là-bas, tu me suivrais.
Sur ton cheval tu me prendrais,
et comme un brave à travers la campagne,
en croupe, tu m'emporterais!
Là-bas, là-bas dans la montagne!

JOSÉ

Carmen!

CARMEN

Là-bas, là-bas, tu me suivrais,
Si tu m'aimais!
Tu n'y dépendrais de personne;
point d'officier à qui tu doives obéir
et point de retraite que sonne

JOSÉ

What are you saying?

CARMEN

No, you don't love me,
no! For if you did,
you'd follow me over there.

JOSÉ

Carmen!

CARMEN

Yes!—
Away over there into the mountains,

JOSÉ

Carmen!

CARMEN

away over there you'd follow me.
You'd take me up behind you on your
horse and like a daredevil you'd carry me
off across the country!
Way over there into the mountains!

JOSÉ

Carmen!

CARMEN

Away over there you'd follow me,
if you loved me!
There you'd not be dependent on anyone;
there'd be no officer you had to obey,
and no Retreat sounding

pour dire à l'amoureux
qu'il est temps de partir!
Le ciel ouvert, la vie errante,
pour pays l'univers;
et pour loi ta volonté,
et surtout la chose enivrante
la liberté! la liberté!

JOSÉ
Mon Dieu!

CARMEN
Là-bas, là-bas dans la montagne,

JOSÉ
Carmen!

CARMEN
là-bas, là-bas, si tu m'aimais,

JOSÉ
Tais-toi!

CARMEN
là-bas, là-bas tu me suivrais!
Sur ton cheval te me prendrais ...

JOSÉ
Ah! Carmen! hélas! tais-toi!
tais-toi! mon Dieu!

CARMEN
et comme un brave, à travers la campagne,
our, tu m'emporterais, si tu m'aimais.

to tell a lover
that it is time to go!
The open sky, the wandering life,
the whole wide world your domain;
for law your own free will,
and above all, that intoxicating thing
Freedom! Freedom!

JOSÉ
Oh God!

CARMEN
Away over there into the mountains,

JOSÉ
Carmen!

CARMEN
away over there, if you loved me,

JOSÉ
Stop it!

CARMEN
away over there you'd follow me!
You'd take me up on your horse ...

JOSÉ
Ah, Carmen! Alas! Stop!
stop! Oh God!

CARMEN
and like a daredevil
you'd carry me off
across the country, if you loved me.

JOSÉ

Hélas! Hélas!

CARMEN

Our, n'est-ce pas,

là-bas, là-bas tu me suivras,

tu m'aimes et tu me suivras!

Là-bas, là-bas emporte-moi!

JOSÉ

Pitié! Carmen! Pitié!

O mon Dieu, hélas!

Ah! Tais-toi! Tais-toi!

Non! Je ne veux plus t'eécouter!

Quitter mon drapeau … déserter …

c'est la honte, c'est l'infamie!

Je n'en veux pas!

CARMEN

Eh bien, pars!

JOSÉ

Carmen, je t'en prie!

CARMEN

Non, je ne t'aime plus!

JOSÉ

Ecoute!

CARMEN

Va! Je te hais!

Adieu! Mais adieu pour jamais!

JOSÉ

Alas! Alas!

CARMEN

Yes, isn't it so,

you will follow me there,

you love me and you'll follow me!

Take me away over there!

JOSÉ

Pity, Carmen! Have pity!

Oh God, alas!

Ah, stop, stop!

No! I won't listen to you!

To abandon my colours … to desert …

that's shameful, that's dastardly!

I'll have none of it!

CARMEN

All right then, go!

JOSÉ

Carmen, I implore you!

CARMEN

No, I don't love you any more!

JOSÉ

Listen!

CARMEN

Go! I hate you!

Good-bye! And good-bye forever!

JOSÉ	**JOSÉ**
Eh bien, soit … adieu, adieu pour jamais!	All right, so be it … good-bye forever!

CARMEN	**CARMEN**
Va-t'en!	Get out!

JOSÉ	**JOSÉ**
Carmen! Adieu! Adieu pour jamais!	Carmen! Goodbye, good-bye forever!

CARMEN	**CARMEN**
Adieu!	Good-bye!

Don José hurries towards the door; just as he reaches it, somebody knocks.

SCENE SEVENTEEN
Finale

DISC NO. 2/TRACK 4

Holà Carmen! Holà! Holà! **In the second-act finale, just as the smugglers arrive to collect Carmen, Zuniga blunders in, looking for Carmen. He is held captive, leaving Don José no recourse but to join the smugglers. The "Là-bas" melody (03:51) returns with militancy, for an entire band of smugglers is now gathering, transforming Carmen's insinuating siren song into a galloping hymn to the rogue's life and bringing the act to an end.**

ZUNIGA *(au dehors)*	**ZUNIGA** *(outside)*
Holà! Carmen! Holà! Holà!	Hallo there, Carmen! Hallo! Hallo!

JOSÉ	**JOSÉ**
Qui frappe? qui vient là?	Who's that knocking? Who's there?

CARMEN	**CARMEN**
Tais-toi! Tais-toi!	Keep quiet!

ZUNIGA

forcing the door

J'ouvre moi-même et j'entre.

sees Don José—to Carmen

Ah! fi, ah! fi, la belle!
Le choix n'est pas heureux; c'est se mésallier
de prendre le soldat quand on a l'officier.

to Don José

Allons! Décampe!

JOSÉ
Non!

ZUNIGA
Si fait, tu partiras!

JOSÉ
Je ne partirai pas!

ZUNIGA

striking him

Drôle!

JOSÉ

drawing his sword

Tonnerre! Il va pleuvoir des coups!

ZUNIGA

I'm opening up myself, and coming in.

Ah! Fi, fi! My lovely lady!
This isn't a happy choice; it's demeaning
to take the soldier when you've got the officer.

Off with you, get moving!

JOSÉ
No!

ZUNIGA
You certainly will go!

JOSÉ
I shall not go!

ZUNIGA

Scoundrel!

JOSÉ

By thunder! It's going to rain blows!

CARMEN

throwing herself between them

Au diable le jaloux! *(appelant)*
A moi! A moi!

Gypsies appear from all sides. Carmen points to Zuniga. Dancaïro and Remendado hurl themselves upon him and disarm him.

CARMEN

Bel officier! Bel officier, l'amour
vous joue en ce moment un assez vilain
tour.
Vous arrivez fort mal, hélas! Et nous
sommes forcés,
ne voulant être dénoncés,
de vous garder au moins ... pendant une
heure.

LE DANCAÏRE ET LE REMENDADO

Mon chere monsieur,
nous allons, s'il vous plaît,
quitter cette demeure;
vous viendrez avec nous?

CARMEN

C'est une promenade.

LE DANCAÏRE ET LE REMENDADO

Consentez-vous?

TOUS LES BOHÉMIENS

Répondez, camarade.

CARMEN

Devil take the jealous! *(calling)*
Help! Help!

CARMEN

My fine officer! My fine officer, love
at the moment is playing you a rather dirty
trick.
Your arrival is most untimely; and alas,
we are compelled,
not wishing to be betrayed, to detain you
... for at least an hour.

EL DANCAÏRO AND EL REMENDADO

My dear sir,
if you please, we are going to leave this
establishment;
you'll come with us?

CARMEN

Just for a stroll.

EL DANCAÏRO AND EL REMENDADO

Do you consent?

ALL THE GYPSIES

Answer, comrade.

ZUNIGA

Certainement,

d'autant plus que votre argument

est un de ceux auxquels on ne résiste guère,

mais gare à vous! Gare à vous plus tard!

ZUNIGA

Certainly,

the more so since your argument

is one of those that can hardly be resisted;

but take care! Look out for yourselves later!

LE DANCAÏRE

La guerre, c'est la guerre!

En attendant, mon officier,

passez devant sans vous faire prier!

EL DANCAÏRO

War is war!

Meantime, my good sir,

carry on without further argument!

LE REMENDADO ET LES BOHÉMIENS

Passez devant sans vous faire prier!

EL REMENDADO AND THE GYPSIES

Carry on without further argument!

The officer is led out by four gypsies armed with pistols.

CARMEN *(à Don José)*

Es-tu des nôtres maintenant?

CARMEN *(to Don José)*

Are you one of us now?

JOSÉ

Il le faut bien.

JOSÉ

I have no alternative.

CARMEN

Ah! Le mot n'est pas galant,

mais qu'importe, va, tu ty feras

quand tu verras

comme c'est beau, la vie errante;

pour pays, l'univers,

et pour loi ta volonté,

et surtout, la chose, enivrante

la liberté! La liberté!

CARMEN

Ah! that's not gallantly put,

but no matter, go, you'll take to it there

when you see

how fine is the wandering life;

the whole world your domain,

your own free will for law,

and above all that intoxicating thing

Freedom! Freedom!

TOUS *(à Don José)*

Suis-nous à travers la campagne,

viens avec nous dans la montagnen,

ALL *(to Don José)*

Take to the country with us,

come with us into the mountains,

suis-nous et tu t'y feras
quand tu verras, là-bas,
comme c'est beau, la vie errante;
pour pays, l'univers,
et pour loi, ta volonté!
Et surtout, la chose enivrante
la liberté! La liberté!
Le ciel ouvert, la vie errante,
pour pays tout l'univers;
pour loi ta volonté,
et surtout la chose enivrante:
la liberté, La liberté!

come with us and you'll take to it there
when you see, away over there;
how fine is the wandering life:
the whole world your domain,
your own free will for law!
And above all that intoxicating thing
Freedom! Freedom!
The open sky, the wandering life,
the whole wide world your domain;
your own free will for law,
and above all that intoxicating thing
Freedom! Freedom!

ENTR'ACTE

Act 3

SCENE EIGHTEEN
Introduction

The curtain rises on a wild and rocky scene; the night is dark and the solitude complete. During the musical prelude a smuggler appears at the top of the rocks, then another, then two more, and finally twenty here and there, climbing and scrambling over the rocks. Some of them are carrying heavy bales on their shoulders.

DISC NO. 2/TRACK 5

Entr'acte One of Bizet's most beautiful melodies appears in the entr'acte, apropos of nothing really—a soaring flute solo heard over arpeggios in the harp. The melody is never heard again but it effectively removes the audience from the bustle of Seville, placing the action in the country and perhaps reflecting Don José's sad reminiscence of happier times.

DISC NO. 2/TRACK 6

The smugglers appear singing a hushed chorus with a tinge of melancholy exhaustion.

CHOEUR	**CHORUS**
Ecoute, écoute, compagnon, écoute,	Listen, friend, listen,
la fortune est là-bas, là-bas,	fortune lies over there,
mais prends garde pendant la route,	but take care along the way,
prends garde de faire un faux pas!	and watch your step!

LE DANCAÏRE, LE REMENDADO, JOSÉ, CARMEN, MERCÉDÈS ET FRASQUITA	**EL DANCAÏRO, EL REMENDADO, JOSÉ, CARMEN, MERCÉDÈS AND FRASQUITA**
Notre métier est bon,	Our calling is a good one,
mais pour le faire il faut	but to follow it you must
avoir une âme forte!	have a stout heart!

Et le péril est en haut, il est en bas,	There's danger up above, and down below,
il est partout, qu'importe!	it's everywhere—what of it!
Nous allons devant nous	We go forward
sans souci du torrent,	without worrying about the torrent,
san souci de l'orage,	without worrying abut the storm,
san souci du soldat	without worrying about the soldier
qui là-bas nous attend,	who's waiting for us over there,
et nous guette au passage—	and keeping a sharp lookout for us—
sans souci nous allons en avant!	we go forward without worrying!

TOUS

Ecoute, compagnon, écoute, *etc.*

ALL

Listen, friend, listen, *etc.*

LE DANCAÏRE

Halte! Nous allons nous arrêter ici … ceux qui ont sommeil pourront dormir pendant une demi-heure.

EL DANCAÏRO

Halt! We're going to stop here … those who feel sleepy can doss down for half an hour.

LE REMENDADO

stretching himself out voluptuously

Ah!

EL REMENDADO

Ah!

DISC NO. 2/TRACK 7

LE DANCAÏRE

Je vais, moi, voir s'il y a moyen de faire entrer les marchandises dans la ville … une brèche s'est faite dans le mur d'enceinte et nous pourrions passer par là.

calling out

Remendado!

EL DANCAÏRO

Me, I'm going to see if there's some way of getting the stuff into the town … a gap has been made in the outer wall and we could get through that way.

Remendado!

LE REMENDADO	EL REMENDADO
waking up	
Hé?	Hé?

LE DANCAÏRE	EL DANCAÏRO
Debout, tu vas venir avec moi.	Get up, you're coming with me.

LE REMENDADO	EL REMENDADO
Mais, patron …	But, boss …

LE DANCAÏRE	EL DANCAÏRO
Qu'est-ce que c'est?	What's that?

LE REMENDADO	EL REMENDADO
getting up	
Voilà, patron, voilà!	Here we are, boss, here!

LE DANCAÏRE	EL DANCAÏRO
Allons, passe devant.	Right, go on ahead.

LE REMENDADO	EL REMENDADO
Et moi qui rêvais que j'allais pouvoir dormir … C'était un rêve, hélas! c'était un rêve!	And I who thought I was going to be able to sleep … It was a dream, alas, it was a dream!

He goes out, followed by Dancaïro. During this scene between Carmen and Don José, a few gypsy men light a fire, by which Mercédès and Frasquita come and sit down; the others roll themselves up in their cloaks, lie down and go to sleep.

JOSÉ	JOSÉ
Voyons, Carmen … si je t'ai parlé trop durement, je t'en demande pardon faisons la paix.	Look, Carmen … if I spoke to you too harshly, I ask your forgiveness. Let's make up.

CARMEN

Non.

JOSÉ

Tu es le diable, Carmen?

CARMEN

Oui, qu'est-ce que tu regardes là, à quoi penses-tu?

JOSÉ

Je me dis que là-bas il y a une bonne vieille femme qui croit que je suis encore un honnête homme …

CARMEN

Une bonne vieille femme?

JOSÉ

Oui; ma mère.

CARMEN

Ta mère. Eh bien, tu ne ferais pas mal d'aller la retrouver.

JOSÉ

Carmen, si tu me parles encore de nous séparer …

CARMEN

Tu me tuerais, peut-être?

José does not answer

CARMEN

No.

JOSÉ

You're worried, Carmen?

CARMEN

Yes, what's that you're looking at there, what are you thinking of?

JOSÉ

I'm telling myself that down there is a good old woman who believes me still to be an honest man …

CARMEN

A good old woman?

JOSÉ

Yes, my mother.

CARMEN

Your mother. Well then, you'd do no harm by going to find her.

JOSÉ

Carmen, if you talk to me any more about us separating …

CARMEN

You would kill me, perhaps?

A la bonne heure … Mêlons! Coupons! (Card Trio) **This is the moment that, for Carmen, is the crux of the action in the opera. Frasquita and Mercédès are playing with tarot cards. When Carmen tries her hand, the cards reveal her dire fate (03:27) She is hurtling toward death, and there is nothing she can do about it. She is devastated and almost instantly resigned to what seems inevitable. The section of the scene beginning with "En vain pour éviter les réponses amères" (04:05) reveals her fatalistic attitude in a mournful melody that develops with the same staggering intensity as the fate motive. It is perhaps the most substantial and beautiful solo moment Carmen has in the entire opera.**

CARMEN

A la bonne heure … J'ai vu dans les cartes
que nous devions finir ensemble.

JOSÉ

Tu es le diable, Carmen?

CARMEN

Mais oui, je te l'ai déjà dit …

CARMEN

Well and good … I've seen in the cards
that we are to finish together.

JOSÉ

You're worried, Carmen?

CARMEN

Why yes, I've already told you so …

SCENE NINETEEN
Trio

She turns her back on José and goes and sits down by Mercédès and Frasquita. After a moment of indecision, Don José moves off in his turn and goes and stretches himself out upon the rocks. During the final exchanges in the foregoing scene, Mercédès and Frasquita have been spreading out playing cards in front of them.

FRASQUITA ET MERCÉDÈS

Mêlons! Coupons!
Bien, c'est cela!
Trois cartes ici …

FRASQUITA AND MERCÉDÈS

Shuffle! Cut!
Good, that's that!
Three cards here …

Quatre là!
Et maintenant, parlez, mes belles,
de l'avenir, donnez-nous des nouvelles;
dites-nous qui nous trahira,
dites-nous qui nous aimera!
Parlez, parlez!

FRASQUITA
Moi, je vois un jeune amoureux,
qui m'aime on ne peut davantage.

MERCÉDÈS
Les mien est très riche et très vieux,
mais il parle de mariage.

FRASQUITA
Je me campe sur son cheval,
et dans la montagne il m'entraîne.

MERCÉDÈS
Dans un château presque royal,
le mien m'installe en souveraine!

FRASQUITA
De l'amour à n'en plus finir,
tous les jours, nouvelles folies!

MERCÉDÈS
De l'or tant, que j'en puis tenir,
des diamants, des pierreries!

FRASQUITA
Le mien devient un chef fameux,
cent hommes marchent à sa suite!

four there!
And now speak, my lovelies,
give us news of the future;
tell us who's going to betray us,
tell us who's going to love us!
Speak! Speak!

FRASQUITA
Me, I see a young suitor,
no one could love me more.

MERCÉDÈS
Mine is very rich and very old,
but he talks of marriage.

FRASQUITA
I settle myself firmly on his horse
and he carries me off into the mountains.

MERCÉDÈS
In an almost royal castle
mine installs me in queenly state!

FRASQUITA
Never-ending love,
every day new raptures!

MERCÉDÈS
As much gold as I can take,
diamonds, precious stones!

FRASQUITA
Mine becomes a famous leader,
a hundred men march in his train!

MERCÉDÈS

Le mien en croirai-je mes yeux?

Oui … il meurt!

Ah! je suis veuve et j'hérite!

REPRISE DE L'ENSEMBLE

Parlez encor, parlez, mes belles, etc.

They begin to consult the cards again.

MERCÉDÈS

Fortune!

FRASQUITA

Amour!

CARMEN

Voyons, que j'essaie à mon tour.

She starts to turn up the cards.

Carreau, pique … la mort!

J'ai bien lu … moi d'abord.

Ensuite lui … pour tous les deux la mort!

in a low voice, while continuing to shuffle the cards

En vain pour éviter les réponses amères,

en vain tu mêleras;

cela ne sert à rien, les cartes

sont sincères et ne mentiront pas!

Dans le livre d'en haut

si ta page est heureuse,

mêle et coupe sans peur,

la carte sous tes doigts se tournera joyeuse,

MERCÉDÈS

Mine … can I believe my eyes?

Yes … he dies

Ah! I'm a widow and I inherit!

TOGETHER REPRISE

Speak again, speak, my lovelies, etc.

MERCÉDÈS

Fortune!

FRASQUITA

Love!

CARMEN

Let's see—let me have a try.

Diamond, spade … Death!

I read it clearly … me first.

Then him … for both of us, Death!

In vain to avoid bitter replies,

in vain will you shuffle;

that achieves nothing, the cards

are truthful and will not lie!

If your page in the book

up above is a happy one,

shuffle and cut without fear,

the card under your fingers will turn up

t'annonçant le bonheur.
Mais si tu dois mourir,
si le mot redoutable
est écrit par le sort,
recommence vingt fois, la carte impitoyable
répétera la mort!

nicely, foretelling good luck.
But if you are to die,
if the terrible word
has been written by Destiny,
begin twenty times—the pitiless card
will repeat Death!

turning up the cards

Encor! Encor! Toujours la mort!

Again! Always Death!

FRASQUITA ET MERCÉDÈS
Parlez encor, parlez mes belles, etc.

FRASQUITA AND MERCÉDÈS
Speak again, my lovelies, speak! etc.

CARMEN
Encore! le désepoir!
Toujours la mort!

CARMEN
Again! Despair!
Always Death!

Dancaïro and Remendado return

CARMEN
Eh bien? …

CARMEN
Well? …

LE DANCAÏRE
Eh bien, j'avais raison de ne pas me fier de
Lillas Pastia. Nous avons aperçu trois
douaniers qui gardaient la brèche.

EL DANCAÏRO
Well, I was right not to trust Lillas Pastia.
We spotted three customs men guarding
the gap.

CARMEN *(en riant)*
N'ayez pas peur, Dancaïre, nous vous en
répondrons de vos trois douaniers …

CARMEN *(laughing)*
Have no fear, Dancaïro, we'll take care of
your three customs men for you …

JOSÉ *(furieux)*
Carmen!

JOSÉ *(furious)*
Carmen!

LE DANCAÏRE

Ah! tu vas nous laisser tranquilles avec ta
jalousie. Tu vas te placer là, sur cette hau-
teur. Dans le cas où tu apercevrais
quelqu'un, passes ta colère sur l'indiscret.
En route alors …

to the women

Mais vous me répondrez vraiment de ces
trois douaniers?

CARMEN

N'ayez pas peur, Dancaïre.

EL DANCAÏRO

Ah, you will give us a rest from your jeal-
ousy. You will post yourself there on that
height. If you should happen to spot anyone, take your anger out on such an ill-
advised person. On our way, then …

But you really will answer to me for these
three customs men?

CARMEN

Have no fear, Dancaïro.

DISC NO. 2/TRACK 9

**As the three women go to distract the customs official with their charms, they sing a jaunty
counterpoint that inspires the chorus to join in a risqué parody of an operatic call-to-arms.**

SCENE TWENTY
Ensemble with Chorus

CARMEN, MERCÉDÈS ET FRASQUITA

Quant au douanier, c'est notre affaire,
tout comme un autre il aime à plaire,
il aime à faire le galant;
ah! laissez-nous passer en avant!

TOUTES LES FEMMES

Quant au douanier, c'est notre affaire, *etc.*

CARMEN, MERCÉDÈS AND FRASQUITA

As for the customs man, he's our affair;
just like the next man he loves to please,
he loves to play the gallant;
ah! leave us to go on ahead!

ALL THE GIRLS

As for the customs man, he's our affair, *etc.*

TOUS	**EVERYONE**
Il aime à plaire!	He loves to please!
MERCÉDÈS	**MERCÉDÈS**
Le douanier sera clément!	The customs man will be easy on us!
TOUS	**EVERYONE**
Il est galant!	He is gallant!
CARMEN	**CARMEN**
Le douanier sera charmant!	The customs man will be charming!
TOUS	**ALL**
Il aime à plaire!	He loves to please!
MERCÉDÈS	**MERCÉDÈS**
Le douanier sera galant!	The customs man will be gallant!
FRASQUITA	**FRASQUITA**
Oui, le douanier sera même entreprenant!	Yes, the customs man will even be forward!
TOUS	**ALL**
Oui, le douanier c'est notre/leur affaire,	Yes, the customs man is our/their affair;
tout comme un autre il aime à plaire,	just like the next man he loves to please,
il aime à faire le galant,	he loves to play the gallant;
laissez-nous/les passer en avant!	let us/them go on ahead!
CARMEN, MERCÉDÈS ET FRASQUITA	**CARMEN, MERCÉDÈS AND FRASQUITA**
Il ne s'agit plus de bataille,	It's no longer a question of battle;
non, il s'agit tout simplement	no, it's simply a question
de se laisser prendre la taille	of letting ourselves be taken by the waist
et d'écouter un compliment.	and listening to a compliment.
S'il faut aller jusqu'au sourire,	If it's necessary to go as far as a smile,
que voulez-vous, on sourira!	what of it?—we'll smile!

TOUTES LES FEMMES

Et d'avance, je puis le dire,
la contrebande passera!
En avant! Marchons! Allons!

ALL THE WOMEN

And here and now I can say
the stuff will get through!
Forward! On our way! Let's go!

TOUT LE MONDE

Oui, le douanier c'est notre/leur affaire, *etc.*

ALL

Yes, the customs man is our/their affair, *etc.*

Everyone leaves, Don José brings up the rear, examining the priming of his carbine; just before he disappears, a man is seen moving behind a rock. It is Micaëla's guide. The guide advances cautiously, then signals to Micaëla that the coast is clear.

DISC NO. 2/TRACK 10

LE GUIDE

Nous y sommes.

THE GUIDE

We're there.

MICAËLA MICAËLA

entering

C'est ici.

MICAËLA

This is the place.

LE GUIDE

Oui, vilain endroit, n'est-ce pas, et pas rassurant du tout?

THE GUIDE

Yes, nasty spot, isn't it, and not at all reassuring?

MICAËLA

Je ne vois personne.

MICAËLA

I don't see anybody.

LE GUIDE

Ils reviendront bientôt. Ils n'ont pas emporté toutes leurs marchandises … prenez garde … l'un de leurs doit être en sentinelle et si l'on nous apercevrait …

THE GUIDE

They'll come back soon, for they haven't taken away all their goods … take care … one of their men must be on sentry–go, and if we were seen …

MICAËLA

Je l'espère bien qu'on m'apercevra …
puisque je suis venue ici justement pour
parler à un de ces contrebandiers …

LE GUIDE

Eh bien, vous pouvez vous vanter d'avoir
du courage … venir ainsi affronter ces
Bohémiens …

MICAËLA

Je n'aurais pas peur, je vous assure.

LE GUIDE

Bien vrai?

MICAËLA

Bien vrai.

LE GUIDE *(naïvement)*

Alots je vous demanderai la permission de
m'en aller. Si ça ne vous fait rien, j'irai vous
attendre à l'auberge au bas de la montagne.
Vous restez décidément?

MICAËLA

I sincerely hope someone will see me …
since that's just what I've come here for, to
speak to one of these smugglers …

THE GUIDE

Well now, you can boast of having courage
… to come here like this to face these gypsies …

MICAËLA

I shouldn't be afraid, I assure you.

THE GUIDE

Truly?

MICAËLA

Truly.

THE GUIDE *(naïvely)*

Then I'll ask your permission to take
myself off. If it's all the same to you I'll go
and wait for you in the inn at the foot of
the mountain.
You're determined to stay?

DISC NO. 2/TRACK 11

Oui, je reste! … Je dis que rien ne m'épouvante (Micaëla's Air) At this depressing point in the opera,
the air Bizet wrote for Micaëla is always welcome. It is an elegant, glowing testament to her
faith in her love for Don José (00:27). Like the first-act duet, it would not be out of place in an
opera of Gounod or Massenet. The orchestration is particularly effective, with a prominent
role given to the evocative and reflective French horn. The melody is borne on the swirling
arpeggios in the cellos, as if to suggest the uncertainty that surrounds her unshakable fidelity
to her beloved.

Hilde Gueden, an Austrian lyric soprano as Micaëla.

MICAËLA

Oui, je reste!

LE GUIDE

Que tous les saints du paradis vous soient en aide alors, mais c'est une drôle idée que vous avez là …

MICAËLA

looking around her

Mon guide avait raison … l'edroit n'est pas bien rassurant.

MICAËLA

Yes. I'm staying!

THE GUIDE

May all the saints in paradise come to your aid then, but it's a funny idea you've got there …

MICAËLA

My guide was right … it's not a very reassuring spot.

SCENE TWENTY-ONE
Aria

MICAËLA

Je dis, que rien ne m'épouvante,
je dis, hélas! que je réponds de moi;

MICAËLA

I say that nothing frightens me, I say, alas,
that I have only myself to depend on;

mais j'ai beau faire la vaillante,	but I have tried in vain to be brave,
au fond du coeur, je meurs d'effroi!	at heart I'm dying of fright!
Seule en ce lieu sauvage,	Alone in this wild place,
toute seule j'ai peur,	all alone, I'm afraid,
mais j'ai tort d'avoir peur;	but I do wrong to be afraid;
vous me donnerez du courage,	you will give me courage
vous me protégerez, Seigneur.	you will protect me, Lord.
Je vais voir de près cette femme	I shall get a close look at this woman
dont les artifices maudits	whose evil wiles
ont fini par faire un infâme	have finished by making a criminal
de celui que j'amais jadis	of the man I once loved
elle est dangereuse, elle est belle,	she is dangerous, she is beautiful,
mais je ne veux pas avoir peur,	but I won't be afraid,
je parlerai haut devant elle.	I shall speak out in front of her,
Ah! Seigneur,	Ah! Lord,
vous me protégerez!	you will protect me!
Ah! je dis, que rien ne m'épouvante, *etc.*	Ah! I say that nothing will frighten me, *etc.*
… protégez-moi, O Seigneur,	… protect me, O Lord,
Protégez-moi, Seigneur!	protect me, Lord!
Mais … je ne me trompe pas … sur ce	But … I'm not mistaken … on that
rocher, c'est Don José.	rock—it's Don José.

calling out

José! José! José! José!   José! José! José! José!

Terrified

DISC NO. 2/TRACK 12

Mais … je ne me trompe pas Micaëla hides when she sees Don José fire his gun at a figure who turns out to be Escamillo. The air is thick with testosterone in the vigorous duet that follows (00:34), in which Don José boldly challenges the man he sees as his rival while Escamillo—obviously a far more skilled fighter—is amused by his passion. Though the second half of the duet is often cut, it is heard in its entirety here (02:23), revealing that Escamillo spares Don José's life when he has the better of him, even though Don José was ready to kill him.

Mais que fait-il? … Il arme sa carabine, il ajuste … il fait feu.

But what is he doing? … He's cocking his carbine … he's aiming … he fires.

A shot is heard.

Ah! mon Dieu, j'ai trop présumé de mon courage …

Ah, my God, I overestimated my courage …

She disappears behind the rocks. At the same moment Escamillo comes in, holding his hat in his hand.

ESCAMILLO

Quelques lignes plus bas, et ce n'est pas moi qui aurais le plaisir de combattre les taureaux que je suis en train de conduire …

ESCAMILLO

A little lower … and it isn't I who would have the pleasure of fighting the bulls I'm about to drive …

Enter José

JOSÉ

carrying his cloak

Qui êtes-vous? Répondez.

JOSÉ

Who are you? Answer.

ESCAMILLO

very calm

Eh là … doucement!

ESCAMILLO

Eh eh … gently!

SCENE TWENTY-TWO
Duet

ESCAMILLO

Je suis Escamillo, Torero de Grenade!

ESCAMILLO

I'm Escamillo, the Granada matador!

JOSÉ

Escamillo!

JOSÉ

Escamillo!

ESCAMILLO

C'est moi!

ESCAMILLO

That's me!

JOSÉ

JOSÉ

returning his knife to its sheath

Je connais votre nom,

soyez le bienvenu; mais vraiment, camarade,

vous pouviez y rester.

I know your name,

you're welcome; but truly, comrade,

that could have been the end of you.

ESCAMILLO

Je ne vous dis pas non,

mais je suis amoureux, mon cher, à la folie,

et celui-là serait un pauvre compagnon,

qui, pour voir ses amours, ne risquerait sa vie!

ESCAMILLO

I'm not denying it, but, my friend, I am

madly in love,

and he would be a wretched fellow

who wouldn't risk his live to see his ladylove!

JOSÉ

Celle que vous aimez est ici?

JOSÉ

The girl you love is here?

ESCAMILLO

Justement.

C'est une zingara, mon cher.

ESCAMILLO

Exactly.

She's a gypsy girl, my friend.

JOSÉ

Elle s'appelle?

JOSÉ

Her name?

ESCAMILLO
Carmen.

JOSÉ
Carmen!

ESCAMILLO
Carmen! oui, mon cher.
Elle avait pour amant
un soldat qui a déserté pour elle.
Ils s'adoraient, mais c'est fini, je crois.
Les amours de Carmen ne durent pas
six mois.

JOSÉ
Vous l'aimez cependant!

ESCAMILLO
Je l'aime!
Oui, mon cher, je l'aime à la folie!

JOSÉ
Mais pour nous enlever nos filles de
bohème, savez-vous bien qu'il faut payer?

ESCAMILLO
Soit! On paiera.

JOSÉ
Et que le prix se paie à coups de navaja!

ESCAMILLO
A coups de navaja!

JOSÉ
Comprenez-vous?

ESCAMILLO
Carmen.

JOSÉ
Carmen!

ESCAMILLO
Carmen! Yes, my friend.
She had as a lover
a soldier who once deserted on her account.
They adored each other, but it's over, I think.
Carmen's affairs don't last six months.

JOSÉ
Yet you love her!

ESCAMILLO
I love her!
Yes, my friend, I love her to distraction!

JOSÉ
But to take our gypsy girls away from us
you know that you have to pay?

ESCAMILLO
All right! I'll pay.

JOSÉ
And that the price is paid with the knife!

ESCAMILLO
With the knife!

JOSÉ
You understand?

ESCAMILLO

Le discours est très net.

Ce déserteur, ce beau soldat qu'elle aime,

ou du moins qu'elle aimait—

c'est donc vous?

JOSÉ

Oui, c'est moi-même!

ESCAMILLO

J'en suis ravi, mon cher,

et le tour est complet!

Both draw their knives and wrap their left arm in their cloaks.

JOSÉ

Enfin ma colère

trouve à qui parler!

Le sang, je l'espère,

va bientôt couler, *etc.*

ESCAMILLO

Quelle maladresse,

j'en rirais vraiment!

Chercher la maîtresse

et trouver l'amant! *etc.*

ENSEMBLE

Mettez-vous en garde,

et veillez sur vous!

Tant pis pour qui tarde

à parer les coups!

En garde! Allons! Veillez sur vous!

They take up positions on guard at some distance from each other.

ESCAMILLO

You put it very clearly.

This deserter, this fine soldier she loves,

or rather, used to love—

is you, then?

JOSÉ

Yes, myself!

ESCAMILLO

I'm delighted, my friend,

and the wheel's come full circle!

JOSÉ

At last my rage has found an outlet!

Blood, I hope,

will soon flow, *etc.*

ESCAMILLO

What a predicament,

I could laugh at it, really!

To look for the mistress

and find the lover! *etc.*

TOGETHER

Put up your guard,

and look out for yourself!

So much the worse for the one

who's slow at parrying!

On guard! Come on! Look out for yourself!

ESCAMILLO	**ESCAMILLO**
Je la connais, ta garde navarraise.	I know it, your Navarrais-style guard,
Et je te previens en ami,	and I warn you, in a friendly way,
Qu'elle ne vaut rien …	that it's no good …

Without answering, Don José advances upon the matador.

A ton aise.	As you like.
Je t'aurai du moins averti.	At least I'll have warned you.

Fight. Incidental music. The matador, very calm, attempts only to defend himself.

JOSÉ	**JOSÉ**
Tu m'épargnes, maudit.	You're not trying, you devil.

ESCAMILLO	**ESCAMILLO**
A ce jeu de couteau	At this knife-play
je suis trop fort pour toi.	I'm too good for you.

JOSÉ	**JOSÉ**
Voyons cela.	Let's see.

A swift and very lively hand-to-hand engagement. Don José finds himself at the mercy of the matador, who does not strike.

ESCAMILLO	**ESCAMILLO**
Tout beau,	Steady,
Ta vie est à moi, mais en somme	your life belongs to me, but in short
j'ai pour métier de frapper le taureau,	my job is to kill bulls,
Non de trouer le coeur de l'homme.	not to bore holes in men's hearts.

JOSÉ	**JOSÉ**
Frappe ou bien meurs … Ceci n'est pas un jeu.	Strike, or die … this isn't a game.

ESCAMILLO	**ESCAMILLO**

disengaging himself

Soit, mais au moins respire un peu.	All right, but at least get your breath.

Reprise of ensemble

JOSÉ	**JOSÉ**
Enfin ma colère	At last my rage
trouve à qui parler *etc.*	has found an outlet, *etc.*

ESCAMILLO	**ESCAMILLO**
Quelle maladresse,	What a predicament,
j'en rirais vraiment! *etc.*	I could laugh at it, really! *etc.*

DISC NO. 2/TRACK 13

All of the opera's dramatic themes, and many of its musical themes, are juxtaposed in the confrontations of this finale. Escamillo's music grows calm after his fight with Don José, and he exits (02:07) to a breezy reprise of the Toreador Song played in the lower strings. Micaëla reappears and attempts to pull José back home with a recap of the most lyrical of the music she sang to him in Act I. Carmen's response elicits an almost psychotic explostion of rage from José (05:00), foreshadowing his music in the final confrontation duet in Act IV. After he leaves, (07:30) there is a final quote of Toreador Song in the distance. All the interpersonal issues of the characters and the forces driving them are thus laid out for the final confrontation in Act IV.

SCENE TWENTY-THREE
Finale

They fight. The matador slips and falls. Enter Carmen and Dancaïro; she rushes forward and stays José's hand. The matador gets to his feet; Remendado, Mercédès, Frasquita, and the smugglers have meanwhile come upon the scene.

CARMEN

Holà, holà! José!

ESCAMILLO

Vrai, j'ai l'âme ravie
que ce soit vous, Carmen, que me sauviez
la vie!
(à Don José)
Quant à toi, beau soldat,
je prendrai ma revanche,
et nous jouerons la belle,
le jour où tu voudras reprendre le combat!

LE DANCAÏRE

C'est bon, c'est bon, plus querelle!
Nous, nous allons partir.

to Escamillo

Et toi, l'ami, bonsoir!

ESCAMILLO

Souffrez au moins qu'avant de vous dire au
revoir, je vous invite tous aux courses de
Séville. Je compte pour ma part y briller de
mon mieux
et qui m'aime y viendra!

to José, who makes a threatening gesture

L'ami, tiens-toi tranquille,
j'ai tout dit et je n'ai plus ici
qu'à faire mes adieux!

CARMEN

Stop, stop, José!

ESCAMILLO

Really, I'm overjoyed
that it should be you, Carmen, who saved
my life!
(to Don José)
As for you, my fine soldier,
I'll take my revenge,
and we'll play for two out of three
whenever you wish to renew the fight!

EL DANCAÏRO

Enough, enough, no more quarreling!
We must get going.

And you, my friend, good night!

ESCAMILLO

Allow me at least, before I say goodbye,
to invite you all to the bullfights at Seville.
I expect to be at my most brilliant there,
and who loves me will come!
to José, who makes a threatening gesture

Friend, keep calm,
I've had my say, and I've nothing more
to do here but make my farewells!

Leisurely exit of Escamillo. Don José tries to attack him but is held back by Dancaïro and Remendado.

JOSÉ *(à Carmen)*
Prends garde à toi, Carmen, je suis las de souffrir!

JOSÉ *(to Carmen)*
Take care, Carmen, I'm weary of suffering!

Carmen answers him with a slight shrug of her shoulders and walks off.

LE DANCAÏRE
En route, en route, il faut partir!

EL DANCAÏRO
Let's get going! We must be off!

TOUS
En route, en route, il faut partir!

ALL
Let's get going! We must be off!

LE REMENDADO
Halte! quelqu'un est là qui cherche à se cacher.

EL REMENDADO
Stop! There's someone there trying to hide!
He brings in Micaëla.

He brings in Micaëla.

CARMEN
Une femme!

CARMEN
A woman!

LE DANCAÏRE
Pardieu, la surprise est heureuse!

EL DANCAÏRO
Lord, a pleasant surprise!

JOSÉ
Micaëla!

JOSÉ
Micaëla!

MICAËLA
Don José!

MICAËLA
Don José!

JOSÉ
Malheureuse!
Que viens-tu faire ici?

JOSÉ
Poor girl!
What are you doing here?

MICAËLA

Moi, je viens te chercher.

Là-bas est la chaumière,

où sans cesse priant

une mère, ta mère,

pleure, hélas sur son enfant.

Elle pleure et t'appelle,

elle pleure et te tend les bras;

tu prendras pitié d'elle,

José, ah! José, tu me suivras!

CARMEN

Va-t'en! Va-t'en! Tu feras bien,

notre métier ne te vaut rien!

JOSÉ

Tu me dis de la suivre?

CARMEN

Oui, tu devrais partir!

JOSÉ

Tu me dis de la suivre

pour que toi, tu puisses courir

après ton nouvel amant!

Non! non vraiment!

Dût-il m'en coûter la vie,

non, Carmen, je ne partirai pas,

et la chaîne qui nous lie

nous liera jusqu'au trépas!

Dût-il m'en coûter la vie, *etc.*

MICAËLA

Ecoute-moi, je t'en prie,

MICAËLA

I've come looking for you.

Down there is the cottage

where, praying unceasingly,

a mother, your mother,

weeps, alas, for her son.

She weeps and calls you,

she weeps and holds out her arms to you;

you will take pity on her,

José, ah José, you will come with me!

CARMEN

Go on! Go on! You'll do well to go;

our business means nothing to you!

JOSÉ

You're telling me to go with her?

CARMEN

Yes, you ought to go!

JOSÉ

You're telling me to go with her

so that you can run after

your new lover!

No! Not likely!

Though it should cost me my life,

no, Carmen, I shall not go away,

and the bond which unites us

shall unite us till death!

Though it should cost me my life, *etc.*

MICAËLA

Listen to me, I implore you,

ta mère te tend les bras,
cette chaîne que te lie,
José, tu la briseras!

**FRASQUITA, MERCÉDÈS,
REMENDADO, DANCAÏRE, CHOEUR**
Il t'en coûtera la vie,
José, si tu ne pars pas,
et la chaîne qui vous lie
se rompra par ton trépas.

JOSÉ *(à Micaëla)*
Laisse-moi!

MICAËLA
Hélas, José!

JOSÉ
Car je suis condamné!

**FRASQUITA, MERCÉDÈS,
REMENDADO, DANCAÏRE, CHOEUR**
José! Prends garde!

JOSÉ *(à Carmen)*
Ah! je te tiens, fille damnée,
je te tiens, et je te forcerai bien
à subir la destinée
qui rive ton sort au mien!
Dût-il m'en coûter la vie,
non, non, non, je ne partirai pas!

CHOEUR
Ah! prends garde, prends garde, Don José!

your mother holds out her arms to you,
that bond which unites you,
José, you will break it!

**FRASQUITA, MERCÉDÈS,
REMENDADO, DANCAÏRO, CHORUS**
It will cost you your life,
José, if you don't go,
and the bond which unites you
will be broken by your death.

JOSÉ *(to Micaëla)*
Leave me!

MICAËLA
Alas, José.

JOSÉ
For I am doomed!

**FRASQUITA, MERCÉDÈS,
REMENDADO, DANCAÏRO, CHORUS**
José! Take care!

JOSÉ *(to Carmen)*
Ah! I've got you, accursed girl,
I've got you, and I shall compel you
to bow to the destiny
that links your fate with mine!
Though it should cost me my life,
no, no, no, I shall not go!

CHORUS
Ah! Take care, take care, Don José!

MICAËLA

Une parole encor, ce sera la dernière.
Hélas! José, ta mère se meurt, et ta mère
ne voudrait pas mourir sans t'avoir pardon-
né.

JOSÉ

Ma mère! Elle se meurt?

MICAËLA

Oui, Don José.

JOSÉ

Partons, ah, partons!
(à Carmen) Sois contente, je pars, mais
nous nous reverrons!

He hurries off with Micaëla.

ESCAMILLO *(au loin)*

Toréador, en guarde! etc.

Don José stops at the back, on the rocks. He hesitates, but, after a moment, goes on his way with Micaëla. Carmen rushes in the direction of the voice. The gypsies take up their bales and prepare to leave.

MICAËLA

One word more, this will be the last.
Alas! José, your mother is dying, and she
doesn't want to die without having forgiven
you.

JOSÉ

My mother! She's dying?

MICAËLA

Yes, Don José.

JOSÉ

Let's go, ah, let's go! *(to Carmen)*
Be satisfied! I'm going, but we shall meet
again!

ESCAMILLO *(in the distance)*

Toreador, on guard! etc.

SCENE TWENTY-FOUR
Chorus

A square in Seville, with the walls of the old arena in the background. The entrance to the ring is closed by a long curtain. A bullfight is about to take place, and there is great excitement. Hawkers move about offering water, oranges, fans, etc.

DISC NO. 2/TRACK 14

Entr'acte **The dramatic and flavorful introduction to the last act places the action squarely back in the city, amid the excitement before a bullfight. The darting, dancing rhythms and the unpredictable flair of the orchestration suggest vivid images that will appear when the curtain rises.**

CHOEUR	**CHORUS**
A deux cuartos! A deux cuartos!	Two cuartos! Two cuartos!
Des éventails pour s'éventer!	Fans to cool yourselves!
Des oranges pour grignotter!	Oranges to nibble!
Le programme avec les détails!	Programme with details!
Du vin! De l'eau! Des cigarettes!	Wine! Water! Cigarettes!
A deux cuartos! A deux cuartos! etc.	Two cuartos! Two cuartos! etc.
Yoyez! A deux cuartos!	Look! For two cuartos!
Señoras et caballeros!	Señoras and caballeros!

ZUNIGA	**ZUNIGA**
Des oranges, vite!	Some oranges, look sharp!

PLUSIEURS MARCHANDS	**SEVERAL FRUITSELLERS**

running up

En voici,	Here you are,
prenez, prenez, mesdemoiselles.	take these, ladies.

UN MARCHAND	**ONE OF THEM**

to Zuniga, who pays

Merci, mon officier, merci.	Thank you, officer, thank you.

LES AUTRES MARCHANDS	**THE OTHERS**
Celles-ci, Señor, sont plus belles.	These ones here, sir, are better.
Des éventails pour s'éventer, *etc.*	Fans to cool yourselves, *etc.*

ZUNIGA	**ZUNIGA**
Holà! des éventails!	Here you! Some fans!

UN BOHÉMIEN	**A GYPSY**

running forward

Voulez-vous aussi des lorgnettes?	Want some opera glasses too?

A scene from the final act
in a production staged by the
San Diego Opera.

A deux cuartos! The opening chorus of Act IV is one of the most exciting moments in opera, as the crowd gathers for the toreador's procession before the bullfight. Finally, after a brief intro-duction, we hear the principal theme that is introduced in the opera's prelude (02:46), as the chorus sings in counterpoint, hailing the spectacle that comes to a grand conclusion at the arrival of Escamillo with Carmen on his arm. Carmen and Escamillo make a subdued yet very public declaration of their love, after which (07:26) Frasquita and Mercédès share their con-cerns with Carmen. Their dialogue is underscored by a curiously melancholy repeated figure in the flutes.

REPRISE DU CHOEUR	**CHORUS** *(reprise)*
A deux cuartos! A deux cuartos!	Two cuartos! Two cuartos!
Voyez! voyez! A deux cuartos! *etc.*	Look! Look! Two cuartos! *etc.*
ZUNIGA	**ZUNIGA**
Qu'avez-vous donc fait de la Carmencita?	But what have you done with Carmencita?
FRASQUITA	**FRASQUITA**
Escamillo est ici, la Carmencita ne doit pas être loin.	Escamillo is here, Carmencita can't be far off.
ZUNIGA	**ZUNIGA**
Ah! c'est Escamillo, maintenant?	Ah! It's Escamillo now?
FRASQUITA	**FRASQUITA**
Et son ancien amoureux José, qu'est-il devenu?	And her former lover Don José, what's become of him?
MERCÉDÈS	**MERCÉDÈS**
Il est libre.	He's at large.
ZUNIGA	**ZUNIGA**
Pour le moment.	For the moment.

FRASQUITA

Je ne serais pas tranquille à la place de
Carmen, je ne serais pas tranquille du tout.

FRASQUITA

I shouldn't feel easy in Carmen's place,
I shouldn't feel easy at all.

From outside loud shuts are heard, trumpet calls, etc. The Cuadrilla is arriving.

SCENE TWENTY-FIVE
Chorus and Scene

CHOEUR

Les voici! Voici la quadreille!
La quadrille des toréros!
Sur les lances le soleil brille!
En l'air toques et sombreros!
Les voici! voici la quadrille,
la quadrille des toréros!
Voici, débouchant sur la place,
voici d'abord, marchant au pas,
l'alguazil à vilaine face!
A bas! à bas! à bas! à bas!
Et puis saluons au passage,
saluons les hardis chulos!
Bravo! viva! gloire au courage!
Voici les hardis chulos!
Voyez les banderilleros!
Voyez quel air de crânerie!
Voyez! voyez! voyez! voyez!
Quel regards, et de quel éclat
étincelle la broderie
de leur costume de combat!
Voici les banderilleros!

CHORUS

Here they come! Here's the cuadrilla!
The toreadors's cuadrilla!
The sun flashes on their lances!
Up in the air with your caps and hats!
Here they are! Here's the cuadrilla,
the toreadors's cuadrilla!
Here, coming into the square
first of all, marching on foot,
is the constable with his ugly mug!
Down with him! Down with him!
And now as they go by
let's cheer the bold chulos!
Bravo! Hurrah! Glory to courage!
Here come the bold chulos!
Look at the banderilleros!
See what a swaggering air!
See them! See them!
What looks, and how brilliantly
the ornaments glitter
on their fighting dress!
Here are the banderilleros!

Un autre quadrille s'avance!	Another cuadrilla's coming!
Voyez les picadors!	Look at the picadors!
Comm ils sont beaux!	How handsome they are!
Comme ils vont du fer de leur lance,	How they'll torment the bull's flanks
harceler le flanc des taureaux!	with the tips of their lances!

At last Escamillo appears, accompanied by a radiant and magnificently dressed Carmen.

L'Espada! Escamillo!	The Matador! Escamillo!
C'est l'Espada, la fine lame,	It's the Matador, the skilled swordsman,
celui qui vient terminer tout,	he who comes to finish things off,
qui paraît à la fin du drame	who appears at the drama's end
et qui frappe le dernier coup!	and strikes the last blow!
Vive Escamillo! ah bravo!	Long live Escamillo! Ah bravo!
Les voici! Voici la quadrille! etc.	Here they are! Here's the cuadrilla! etc.

ESCAMILLO *(à Carmen)* **ESCAMILLO** *(to Carmen)*

Si tu m'aimes, Carmen, tu pourras, tout à l'heure,	If you love me, Carmen, soon
être fière de moi.	you can be proud of me.

CARMEN **CARMEN**

Ah! je t'aime, Escamillo, je t'aime,	Ah! I love you, Escamillo, I love you,
et que je meure si j'ai jamais aimé	and may I die if I have ever loved
quelqu'un autant que toi!	anyone as much as you!

TOUS LES DEUX **TOGETHER**

Ah! je t'aime!	Ah! I love you!
Oui, je t'aime!	Yes, I love you!

LES ALGUAZILS **ALGUAZILS**

Place, place! place au seigneur Alcade!	Make way! Make way for his worship the Mayor!

During a little orchestral march the Mayor enters and crosses the stage, preceded and followed by an escort of constables. Meanwhile Frasquita and Mercédès draw near to Carmen.

FRASQUITA

Carmen, un bon conseil, ne reste pas ici!

CARMEN

Et pourquoi, s'il te plaît?

MERCÉDÈS

Il est là!

CARMEN

Qui donc?

MERCÉDÈS

Lui, Don José!

Dans la foule il se cache; regarde.

CARMEN

Oui, je le vois.

FRASQUITA

Prends garde!

CARMEN

Je ne suis pas femme à trembler devant lui.

Je l'attends, et je vais lui parler.

MERCÉDÈS

Carmen, crois-moi, prends garde!

CARMEN

Je ne crains rien!

FRASQUITA

Prends garde!

FRASQUITA

Carmen, a word of advice, don't stay here!

CARMEN

And why, if you please?

MERCÉDÈS

He's there!

CARMEN

Who?

MERCÉDÈS

Him, Don José!

He's hiding among the crowd; look.

CARMEN

Yes, I see him.

FRASQUITA

Take care!

CARMEN

I'm not a woman to tremble in front of him.

I'm expecting him, and I'll speak to him.

MERCÉDÈS

Carmen, believe me, take care!

CARMEN

I'm not afraid of anything!

FRASQUITA

Take care!

The mayor's cortège has entered the arena. Behind him, the procession of the cuadrilla resumes its march and goes into the ring. The crowd follows … and in withdrawing has revealed Don José, leaving him and Carmen alone downstage.

SCENE TWENTY-SIX
Duet and Final Chorus

DISC NO. 2/TRACK 16

C'est toi! C'est moi! **The spectacular opening and its delicate denouement bring the listener to the greatest pages in the entire score, the final confrontation between Don José and Carmen. The fugitive Don José emerges from the shadows as the magnificently dressed Carmen, barely surprised, awaits her destiny. He is pitiful, crying to her in sobbing phrases (00:55) that he wants another chance to love her. She dismisses him coldly, which only makes him beg more fervently. The melody that he sings to the words "Carmen, il est temps encore" (01:50) reveals the depth of his agony, but Carmen sings the same melody back to him as she denies him, even in the face of death. When Don José realizes that she means what she is saying (03:47), he makes one last desperate attempt to convince her.**

CARMEN	**CARMEN**
C'est toi!	It's you!
JOSÉ	**JOSÉ**
C'est moi!	Yes, me!
CARMEN	**CARMEN**
L'on m'avait avertie	I'd been warned
que tu n'etais pas loin, que tu devais venir;	that you were about, that you might come here;
l'on m'avait même dit de craindre pour ma vie	I was even told to fear for my life,
mais je suis brave et n'ai pas voulu fuir.	but I'm no coward and had no intention of running away.

JOSÉ

Je ne menace pas, j'implore, je supplie;
notre passé, Carmen, je l'oublie.
Oui, nous allons tous deux
commencer une autre vie,
loin d'ici, sous d'autres cieux!

CARMEN

Tu demandes l'impossible,
Carmen jamais n'a menti;
son âme reste inflexible.
Entre elle et toi, tout est fini.
Jamais je n'ai menti;
entre nous, tout est fini.

JOSÉ

Carmen, il est temps encore,
oui, il est temps encore.
O ma Carmen, laisse-moi
te sauver, toi que j'adore,
et me sauver avec toi!

CARMEN

Non, je sais bien que c'est l'heure
je sais bien que tu me tueras;
mais que je vive ou que je meure,
non, non, je ne tu céderai pas!

JOSÉ

Carmen, il est temps encor.
Ô ma Carmen, laisse-moi
te sauver, toi que j'adore;
ah! laisse-moi te sauver
et me sauver avec toi!
O ma Carmen, il est temps encore, *etc.*

JOSÉ

I'm not threatening, I'm imploring,
beseeching; our past, Carmen,—I forget it!
Yes, together we are going to begin
another life,
far from here, under new skies!

CARMEN

You ask the impossible,
Carmen has never lied;
her mind is made up.
Between her and you everything's finished.
I have never lied;
all's over between us.

JOSÉ

Carmen, there is still time,
yes, there is still time.
O my Carmen, let me
save you, you I adore,
and save myself with you!

CARMEN

No, I'm well aware that the hour has come,
I know that you are going to kill me;
but whether I live or die,
no, no, I shall not give in to you!

JOSÉ

Carmen, there is still time,
O my Carmen, let me
save you, you whom I adore;
ah! let me save you
and save myself with you!
O my Carmen, there is still time, *etc.*

CARMEN

Pourquoi t'occuper encore
d'un coeur qui n'est plus à toi?
Non, ce coeur n'est plus à toi!
En vain tu dis "Je t'adore",
tu n'obtiendras rien, non, rien de moi.
Ah! c'est en vain,
tu n'obtiendras rien, rien de moi!

JOSÉ

Tu ne m'aimes donc plus?

Carmen is silent.

Tu ne m'aimes donc plus?

CARMEN

Non, je ne t'aime plus.

JOSÉ

Mais moi, Carmen, je t'aime encore;
Carmen, hélas! moi, je t'adore!

CARMEN

A quoi bon tout cela? que mots superflus!

JOSÉ

Carmen, je t'aime, je t'adore!
Eh bien, s'il le faut, pour te plaire,
je resterai bandit, tout ce que tu voudras—
tout, tu m'entends? Tout!
Mais ne me quitte pas,
ô ma Carmen,
ah! Souviens-toi, souviens-toi du passé!
Nous nous aimions naguère!

CARMEN

Why still concern yourself
with a heart that's no longer yours?
No, this heart no longer belongs to you!
In vain you say "I adore you,"
you'll get nothing, no nothing, from me.
Ah! It's useless,
you'll get nothing, nothing, from me!

JOSÉ

Then you don't love me any more?

Then you don't love me any more?

CARMEN

No, I don't love you any more.

JOSÉ

But I, Carmen, I love you still;
Carmen, alas! I adore you!

CARMEN

What's the good of this? What waste of words!

JOSÉ

Carmen, I love you, I adore you!
All right, if I must, to please you
I'll stay a bandit, anything you like—
anything, do you hear? Anything!
But do not leave me,
O my Carmen,
ah! Remember the past!
We loved each other once!

Ah! Ne me quitte pas, Carmen,
ah, ne me quitte pas!

CARMEN
Jamais Carmen ne cédera!
Libre elle est née et libre elle mourra!

CHOEUR ET FANFARES *(dans le cirque)*
Viva! viva! la course est belle!
Viva! sur le sable sanglant
le taureau, le taureau s'élance!
Voyez! voyez! voyez!
Le taureau qu'on harcèle
en bondissant s'élance, voyez!
Frappé juste, en plein coeur,
voyez! voyez! voyez!
Victoire!

Ah! Do not leave me, Carmen,
ah, do not leave me!

CARMEN
Carmen will never yield!
Free she was born and free she will die!

CHORUS AND FANFARES *(in the arena)*
Hurrah! Hurrah! A grand fight!
Hurrah! Across the bloodstained sand
the bull charges!
Look! Look! Look!
The tormented bull
comes bounding to the attack, look!
Struck true, right to the heart,
Look! Look! Look!
Victory!

During the chorus, Carmen and José remain silent, both listening. Hearing shouts of "Victory!" a cry of delight escapes Carmen. Don José's eyes are fixed upon her. The chorus over, she takes a step towards the main entrance of the ring.

The final confrontation between Carmen and Don José in a production at the Metropolitan Opera.

Où vas-tu? Don José quickly unravels, and the music dizzily and sickeningly reflects the quick, violent action that follows when Carmen tries to escape and go to Escamillo, whose triumph echoes from the arena. The confrontation turns ugly and vicious—Carmen insults Don José with a derisive shout of "Tiens!" (There!) (01:50) when she throws the ring he gave her in his face. Unafraid, she strides confidently toward the arena (01:58) and an enraged Don José steps forward and stabs her to death. As she falls lifeless to the ground—the fate motive triumphant at last in the orchestra (02:22)—he weeps over her, singing of his love as the opera ends on a grim final chord.

JOSÉ	**JOSÉ**
blocking her way	
Où vas-tu?	Where are you going?
CARMEN	**CARMEN**
Laisse-moi!	Leave me alone!
JOSÉ	**JOSÉ**
Cet homme qu'on acclame,	This man they're cheering,
c'est ton nouvel amant!	he's your new lover!
CARMEN	**CARMEN**
Laisse-moi! Laisse-moi!	Leave me alone! Leave me alone!
JOSÉ	**JOSÉ**
Sur mon âme,	By my soul,
tu ne passeras pas,	you won't get past,
Carmen, c'est moi que tu suivras!	Carmen, you will come with me!
CARMEN	**CARMEN**
Laisse-moi, Don José, je ne te suivrai pas.	Let me go, Don José, I'm not going with you.
JOSÉ	**JOSÉ**
Tu vas le retrouver. Dis … tu l'aimes donc?	You're going to him. Tell me … you love him then?

CARMEN

Je l'aime!

Je l'aime, et devant la mort même,

je répéterais que je l'aime!

shouts and fanfares again from the arena

CHOEUR

Viva! La course est belle! *etc.*

JOSÉ

Ainsi, le salut de mon âme,

je l'aurai perdu pour que toi,

pour que tu t'en ailles, infâme,

entre ses bras, rire de moi!

Non, par le sang, tu n'irais pas!

Carmen, c'est moi que tu suivras!

CARMEN

Non! non! jamais!

JOSÉ

Je suis las de te menacer!

CARMEN

Eh bien! Frappe-moi donc, ou laisse-moi

passer!

CHOEUR

Victoire!

JOSÉ

Pour la dernière fois, démon,

veux-tu me suivre?

CARMEN

I love him!

I love him, and in the face of death itself

I would go on saying I love him!

CHORUS

Hurrah! A grand fight! *etc.*

JOSÉ

So I am to lose

my heart's salvation so that you

can run to him, infamous creature,

to laugh at me in his arms!

No, by my blood, you shall not go!

Carmen, you're coming with me!

CARMEN

No! No! Never!

JOSÉ

I'm tired of threatening you!

CARMEN

All right, stab me then, or let me pass!

CHORUS

Victory!

JOSÉ

For the last time, you devil,

will you come with me?

CARMEN

Non! non!

Cette bague autrefois,

tu me l'avais donnée,

tiens!

She throws it away.

JOSÉ

advancing on Carmen, knife in hand

Eh bien, damnée!

Carmen draws back, José following, as fanfares sound again in the ring.

CHOEUR

Toréador, en guarde!

Et songe bien, oui, songe en combattant,

qu'un oeil noir te regarde,

et que l'amour t'attend!

Don José stabs Carmen; she falls dead. The curtains are thrown open and the crowd comes out of the arena.

JOSÉ

Vous pouvez m'arrêter.

C'est moi qui l'ai tuée.

Escamillo appears on the arena steps. Don José throws himself upon Carmen's body.

Ah! Carmen! ma Carmen adorée!

THE END

CARMEN

No! No!

This ring that you

once gave me—

here, take it!

JOSÉ

advancing on Carmen, knife in hand

All right, accursed woman!

CHORUS

Toreador, on guard!

And remember, yes, remember as you fight

that two dark eyes are watching you,

and that love awaits you!

JOSÉ

You can arrest me.

I was the one who killed her!

Ah! Carmen! My adored Carmen!

THE END

PHOTO CREDITS

CARMEN

Giuseppe Verdi

LIBRETTO BY MEILHAC & HALEVY

COMPACT DISC ONE